GUIDE TO
ENGLISH GRAMMAR

By Milton L. Clement

Guide to English Grammar, Second Edition with Answer Key

The Library of Congress has this book cataloged as follows:

Clement, Milton L.
      Guide to English Grammar / Milton L. Clement - 2nd ed.
      Includes Index.
      ISBN 0615570968

ISBN-13: 978-0615570969 *(Guide to English Grammar, Second Edition with Answer Key)*

ISBN-10: 0615570968 *(Guide to English Grammar, Second Edition with Answer Key)*

ISBN-13: 978-0615570990 *(Guide to English Grammar, Second Edition without Answer Key)*

ISBN-10: 0615570992 *(Guide to English Grammar, Second Edition without Answer Key)*

TABLE OF CONTENTS

ACKNOWLEDGMENTS

The second edition of *Guide to English Grammar* was definitely a team effort. Many thanks to the contributing writers and editors for providing their excellent expertise to the book. A special thanks to Paige Harmon, a fantastic copy editor, whose educational experience proved to be a priceless resource. Also, a warm thank you to Jupiter Images for providing wonderful illustrations for the text.

PREFACE

This enjoyable book gives complete grammar instruction allowing students to understand, learn, and review English skills.

While keeping a simple approach to learning, the second edition guides students with clear explanations, real-life examples, and hilarious illustrations.

By the completion of *Guide to English Grammar*, students will be able to:

- ❖ master all the rules of English.
- ❖ completely understand sentence structure.
- ❖ speak and write effectively.
- ❖ avoid common grammar mistakes.
- ❖ approach writing projects, big or small.

This educational text gives students the confidence to succeed in classroom use, business communication, or everyday English.

From individuals who are learning by themselves, to students learning in a school, *Guide to English Grammar* offers a full educational experience to each and every reader.

Chapter 1
Nouns

The *computer* is shocking *her*.

1-1 Nouns, Objects and Subjects

Noun	Definitions:	Examples:
	A noun is a person, place, thing or idea.	**Person:** *Bill Clinton* **Place:** *Washington, DC* **Thing:** *a door* **Idea:** *happiness*
Subject	Most sentences contain a subject. *Subjects* are nouns and they are the topic of the sentence. The subject tells the listener or reader where the action is going. The subject always comes before the verb. The subject is the person, place, thing or idea that is doing the action.	**1.** *Students*(subject) → read(verb). **2.** *Dogs*(subject) → bark(verb).
Object	*Objects* are followed by the verb in the sentence. It is the noun that is receiving the action.	**1.** Students read → *books*(object). **2.** Dogs bark → at *people*(object).

Exercise

Exercise 1: Underline the *nouns* in each sentence.

1. <u>Emily</u> enjoys shopping.

2. Mike works at a restaurant.

3. Sophia likes to listen to music.

4. Jim is going to the mall.

5. Jamie has no mail.

6. Shannon lost the wallet.

7. Michael and Tom are friends.

8. Seth purchased a new computer.

9. Chris owns a business.

10. Ann wants to ride the bike.

11. My cat does not like thunderstorms.

12. The store was out of eggs.

13. Can Luke please have pancakes for breakfast?

14. Mike ordered Jason's birthday present three days ago.

15. How did Mary get gum stuck in Ann's hair again?

16. Mom found the homework on the floor.

17. Did Michelle send Margaret an invitation to the party?

18. Not even the dog would eat the meatloaf.

19. Did Louis hear the teacher?

20. Sophia took the book without asking.

21. Carl made Jessica a sandwich.

Exercise 2: Identify the *subject* and the *object* in each sentence.

1. Tim likes reading books.

    Subject → _Tim_ Object → _books_

2. Tom is going to the store.

    Subject → _____ Object → _____

3. Mary reads many magazines.

    Subject → _____ Object → _____

4. Jack accidentally hit a car.

    Subject → _____ Object → _____

5. Jim needs a laptop.

    Subject → _____ Object → _____

6. Ben loves to go bowling.

    Subject → _____ Object → _____

7. Chris must enter the movie theater.

    Subject → _____ Object → _____

8. Ann completed the work.

    Subject → _____ Object → _____

9. Karen shopped at the mall.

    Subject → _____ Object → _____

10. The gardener dug into the ground.

    Subject → _____ Object → _____

1-2 Vowels and Consonants

Definitions:	Examples:
Vowels are used to help with the pronunciation of words. The vowels in the American alphabet are *A, E, I, O, U* and sometimes *Y* - *(Note: Y can occasionally replace I).*	**1.** R<u>ea</u>d **2.** J<u>u</u>mp **3.** T<u>y</u>pe
Consonants are letters of the alphabet which are not a vowels. The consonants in the American alphabet are *B, C, D, F, G, H, J, K, L, M, N, P, Q, R, S, T, V, W, X, Y* and *Z*.	**1.** <u>T</u>a<u>bl</u>e **2.** <u>W</u>a<u>t</u>er **3.** <u>T</u>ele<u>v</u>isio<u>n</u>

Exercise

Exercise 1: Underline the *vowel(s)* in each sentence.

    1. j <u>u</u> m p

    2. s t a r t

    3. w o m a n

    4. p h o n e

    5. l i g h t

Exercise 2: Underline the *consonant(s)* in each sentence.

    1. <u>p</u> <u>l</u> a <u>t</u> e

    2. p a p e r

    3. d o o r

    4. c u p

    5. w i n d o w

The *runners* race each other.

1-3 Plural Nouns - Final *-s* and *-es*

Rules:	Examples:
The plural form of most nouns are created simply by adding the letter *-s*. More than one apple = *apples* More than one pencil = *pencils* More than one computer = *computers*	**Question:** Do you like *apples?* **Answer:** Yes, I do. **Question:** Can I have two *pencils*? **Answer:** Absolutely. **Question:** What's wrong with their *computers*? **Answer:** I have no idea.
Words that end in *-ch, -x, -s* or *-s*–like sounds will require an *-es* for the plural: More than one fox = *foxes* More than one kiss = *kisses* More than one match = *matches*	**1.** There are many *foxes* in the field today. **2.** My grandmother loves to give me *kisses*. **3.** The soccer team has many *matches*.

Rules:	Examples:
Words that end in **-y**:	**1.** Ba<u>by</u> = I have two *babies*.
When the last <u>two</u> letters of a word are consonants, change the ending to **-ies**.	**2.** Da<u>ddy</u> = Many *daddies* celebrate Father's Day.
More than one *la<u>dy</u>* = *ladies*. (**Example 1 and 2**)	**3.** B<u>oy</u> = The two *boys* went to the store.
When the last <u>two</u> letters of a word end with a vowel followed by a consonant, change the *ending* to **-s**. More than one *t<u>oy</u>* = *toys*. (**Example 3**)	

She is holding her computer with both *hands*.

Exercise

Exercise 1: Change each word to the *plural* form.

1. tax = <u>taxes</u>

2. lion = _____

3. map = _____

4. mix = _____

5. pen = _____

6. box = _____

7. ball = _____

8. chance = _____

9. paper = _____

10. note = _____

Exercise 2: Each word ends in –*y*. Change each word to the *plural* form.

1. mummy = *mummies*

2. family = _____

3. key = _____

4. party = _____

5. berry = _____

6. army = _____

7. day = _____

8. butterfly = _____

9. puppy = _____

10. sky = _____

11. library = _____

12. supply = _____

13. bay = _____

14. valley = _____

15. fly = _____

Chapter 2
Verbs (Part 1)

They *ride* together.

2-1 Verbs

Definitions:	Examples:
Verbs are words that give the sentence action. (**Example 1, 2, 3 and 4**)	1. *Go!*
	2. *Stop!*
Verbs also connect sentences together. (**Example 5 and 6**)	3. Dogs *bark*.
	4. People *talk.*
Predicates are all the words that follow the verb in a sentence. (**Example 7 and 8**)	5. She *is* smart.
	6. They *are* loud.
	7. The men *are riding* a bike.
	8. The students *are talking* to the teacher.

Exercise

| imagine | drink | hop | scare | eat |
| breathe | tickle | tickle | hold | say |

Exercise 1: Imagine you are a world famous doctor, and your newest patient is coming to you because she has had the hiccups for three years and needs a cure. Using the *verbs* in the box, write suggestions for things she can do. Then, write two sentences telling us what you think is the best cure for the hiccups.

1. You should _drink_ pickle juice.

2. _____ a spoonful of sugar.

3. Try to _____ into a paper bag.

4. _____ a bunch of zebras running around.

5. _____ your breath for ten seconds.

6. _____ a tongue twister.

7. Let someone _____ your feet.

8. _____ on one foot for thirty seconds.

9. _____ freshly popped popcorn.

10. Ask someone to _____ you.

11. _____

12. _____

Exercise 2: Underline the *verb* in each sentence.

1. She <u>drives</u> slowly.

2. Mom is a slow driver

3. I mow my lawn frequently.

4. She is a quick walker.

5. She walked to the store quickly.

6. I ran to the school.

7. You must enter the movie theater quietly.

8. She works hard.

9. She is a poor student.

10. They dug deep into the ground.

2-2 Past Tense and Continuous Verbs

Past Tense	Rules:	Examples:
	Verbs that end in **-ed** are actions that happened in the past. These verbs are called *past tense*.	1. *talked* 2. *watched* 3. *looked*
Continuous	Verbs that end in **-ing** are *continuous.* Continuous verbs are actions that continue for a length of time.	1. *hiking* 2. *talking* 3. *writing*

Verbs Ending with -ing and -ed

Verbs that end in **-e**	Rules:	
	FOR -ED - If the word ends with **-e** and you would like to add **-ed**, simply add a **-d** to the end of the word. **FOR -ING -** If the word ends with **-e** and you would like to add **-ing**, take off the **-e** and add **-ing**.	1. *bounce – bounced – bouncing* 2. *change – changed – changing* 3. *fade – faded – fading*

Verbs that end in *-ie*	Rules:	Examples:
	FOR *-ED* - If the word ends with *-ie* and you would like to add *-ed* to make the word past tense, simply add a *-d* to the end of the word. **FOR *-ING*** - If the word ends with *-ie* and you would like to add an *-ing*, simply replace the *-ie* and add *-ying*. **Note:* the *-y* still has the *-ie* sound.	1. *lie – lied – lying* 2. *tie – tied – tying* 3. *die – died – dying*
Verbs that end in *-y*	**FOR *-ED*** - If you are adding an *-ed* to the end of the word: If the word ends with (consonant → *-y*) change the *-y* to *-i* and add *-ed*. **(Example 1)** If the word ends with (vowel → *-y*) simply keep the *-y* and add *-ed*. **(Example 2)** **FOR *-ING*** - If the word ends with *-y* and you would like to add an *-ing*, simply keep the *-y* and add *-ing*.	1. *copy – copied – copying* 2. *employ – employed – employing*

Exercise

Exercise 1: Write the correct *-ed* and *-ing* forms for the following words.

1. *(type)*

   typed, _typing_

2. *(die)*

   _____, _____

3. *(erase)*

   _____, _____

4. *(fry)*

   _____, _____

5. *(play)*

   _____, _____

6. *(cry)*

   _____, _____

7. *(tie)*

   _____, _____

8. *(study)*

   _____, _____

9. *(hurry)*

   _____, _____

10. *(enjoy)*

    _____, _____

He is *learning* how to ride a bike.

2-3 Verbs that End with a Vowel Followed by a Consonant

Rules:	Examples:
If the last <u>three</u> letters of the verb ends with a *consonant* →*vowel* →*consonant*, and it is a <u>one</u>-syllable verb: **1.** Double the consonant and add an **-ed** to make the verb past tense. **2.** Double the consonant and add an **-ing** to make the verb continuous.	<u>**One-syllable words**</u> **1.** *d<u>rag</u>* – dra<u>**gged**</u> – dra<u>**gging**</u> **2.** *s<u>top</u>* – sto<u>**pped**</u> – sto<u>**pping**</u> **3.** *d<u>rop</u>* – dro<u>**pped**</u> – dro<u>**pping**</u> <u>*consonant*</u> →<u>*vowel*</u> →<u>*consonant*</u> *drag:* d = <u>***consonant***</u> | r = <u>***consonant***</u> | a = <u>***vowel***</u> | g = <u>***consonant***</u>
If the last <u>three</u> letters of the verb ends with *vowel* →*vowel* →*consonant*, and it is a <u>one</u>-syllable verb: **1.** Keep the same spelling of the verb, and add an **-ed** to make the verb past tense. **2.** Keep the same spelling of the verb, and add an **-ing** to make the verb continuous.	<u>**One-syllable words**</u> **1.** *dr<u>oop</u>* – droop<u>**ed**</u> – droop<u>**ing**</u> **2.** *l<u>oan</u>* – loan<u>**ed**</u> – loan<u>**ing**</u> <u>*vowel*</u> →<u>*vowel*</u> →<u>*consonant*</u> *loan:* l = <u>***consonant***</u> | o = <u>***vowel***</u> | a = <u>***vowel***</u> | n = <u>***consonant***</u>
If the verb ends with *vowel* →*consonant*, and it is a <u>two</u>-syllable verb: **1.** Add an **-ed** to make the verb past tense. **2.** Add an **-ing** to make the verb continuous.	<u>**Two-Syllable Words**</u> **1.** *op<u>en</u>* – op<u>**ened**</u> – op<u>**ening**</u> **2.** *vis<u>it</u>* – visit<u>**ed**</u> – vis<u>**iting**</u> **3.** *answ<u>er</u>* – answ<u>**ered**</u> – answ<u>**ering**</u> <u>*vowel*</u> →<u>*consonant*</u> *open:* o = <u>***vowel***</u> | p = <u>***consonant***</u> | e = <u>***vowel***</u> | n = <u>***consonant***</u>

Exercise

Exercise 1: Write the correct *-ed* and *-ing* forms for the following words.

1. *(act)*

   <u>acted</u>, <u>acting</u>

2. *(look)*

   _____, _____

3. *(bake)*

   _____, _____

4. *(beg)*

   _____, _____

5. *(continue)*

   _____, _____

6. *(cruise)*

   _____, _____

7. *(edit)*

   _____, _____

8. *(entertain)*

   _____, _____

9. *(equip)*

   _____, _____

10. *(erase)*

    _____, _____

11. *(fan)*

    _____, _____

He *closed* the door on his tie.

12. *(heal)*

   _____, _____

13. *(ignore)*

   _____, _____

Exercise 2: Write the correct *-ing* and *-ed* form for each *verb*.

1. *(rob + -ing)* = <u>robbing</u>

2. *(stop + -ed)* = _____

3. *(begin + -ing)* = _____

4. *(die + -ing)* = _____

5. *(jump + ed)* = _____

6. *(run + -ing)* = _____

7. *(start + -ed)* = _____

8. *(take + -ing)* = _____

9. *(require + -ed)* = _____

10. *(complete + -ed)* = _____

11. *(pop + -ing)* = _____

12. *(chop + -ed)* = _____

2-4 Verbs that End with Two Consonants

Rules:	Examples:
If the verb ends with _consonant_ →_consonant_, simply add the **-ing** or **-ed** ending. <u>Do not</u> change the spelling of the word; just add the correct ending.	1. wo**rk** – wo**rked** – wo**rking** 2. rea**ch** – rea**ched** – rea**ching** 3. wa**sh** – wa**shed** – wa**shing** <u>consonant</u> →<u>consonant</u> work: w = <u>**consonant**</u> | o = <u>**vowel**</u> | r = <u>**consonant**</u> | k = <u>**consonant**</u>

Exercise

Exercise 1: Write the correct -ed and -ing forms for the following words.

1. _(crush)_

    crushed, _crushing_

2. _(drift)_

    _____, _____

3. _(add)_

    _____, _____

4. _(wash)_

    _____, _____

5. _(earn)_

    _____, _____

6. _(stuff)_

    _____, _____

7. *(melt)*

_____, _____

8. *(touch)*

_____, _____

9. *(scratch)*

_____, _____

10. *(invent)*

_____, _____

2-5 Regular and Irregular Verbs

> Verbs have four standard components, *simple form*, *simple past*, *past participle*, and *present participle*.

Regular Verbs: Most verbs are regular. With regular verbs, you never change the base form of the verb. Look at the list below. Notice how *drop* changes to <u>*dropped*</u> when used in the past tense. The base form *drop* never changes.

Simple Form:				
drop	*free*	*visit*	*copy*	*play*
Simple Past:				
dropped	*freed*	*visited*	*copied*	*played*
Past Participle:				
dropped	*freed*	*visited*	*copied*	*played*
Present Participle:				
dropping	*freeing*	*visiting*	*copying*	*playing*

Irregular Verbs: Some verbs are irregular. For irregular verbs, you change the spelling of the verb in order to make the verb past tense or a present participle. *(*The irregular verbs list is in the reference section.)*

Simple Form:				
be	*draw*	*feel*	*write*	*see*
Simple Past:				
was, were	*drew*	*felt*	*wrote*	*saw*
Past Participle:				
been	*drawn*	*felt*	*written*	*seen*
Present Participle:				
being	*drawing*	*feeling*	*writing*	*seeing*

He *watched* his keys fall.

Pronunciation of –ed endings

The pronunciation of *verbs* with an –ed ending have three different ending sounds.

The final –ed is pronounced as a "d" after voiced sounds:

realized	cried	studied	called	dived
brewed	boiled	absorbed	hugged	scrubbed

The final –ed is pronounced as a "t" after voiceless sounds:

hoped	stopped	asked	hopped	wrecked
booked	helped	locked	pushed	walked

The final –ed is pronounced as a "id" after –d and –t:

created	started	waited	counted	extended
exported	inserted	wasted	needed	added

Exercise

Exercise 1: Practice the sentences below by answering *yes* to the following questions. Your answer should be similar to the answer given for the example.

1. Question: Did you walk to school this morning?

    Answer: <u>Yes, I walked to school this morning.</u>

2. Question: Did you write that report?

    Answer: _____

3. Question: Did you jog this morning?

    Answer: _____

4. Question: Did you wreck the car?

    Answer: _____

5. Question: Did he marry her?

    Answer: _____

6. Question: Did he accept the paper?

    Answer: _____

7. Question: Did they win the soccer game?

    Answer: _____

8. Question: Did you understand the material?

    Answer: _____

9. Question: Did you study for the math test?

    Answer: _____

10. Question: Did you hear me?

    Answer: _____

11. Question: Did you know him?

    Answer: _____

Exercise 2: Using the irregular verb list in the reference section, write the *simple past* and *past participle* forms of each word.

1. bite

   <u>bit</u>, <u>bitten</u>

2. break

   _____, _____

3. build

   _____, _____

4. choose

   _____, _____

5. cut

   _____, _____

6. find

   _____, _____

7. forget

   _____, _____

8. freeze

   _____, _____

9. go

   _____, _____

10. know

    _____, _____

He *thought* they liked him.

Chapter 3
Verbs (Part 2)

He *feels* this relationship is not working!

3-1 Nonprogressive / Nonaction Verbs

Definition:	Examples:
Nonprogressive or *nonaction verbs* refer to or describe mental actions. (***Mental Actions****:* emotional, mental and possession) These verbs describe general feelings or actions. Nonprogressive verbs are always written in the simple tense.	1. (*feel*) I *feel* sad about my grandmother dying. 2. (*think*) I *think* I should study before my test tomorrow. 3. (*taste*) The pizza *tastes* great. 4. (*smell*) The bakery *smells* great. 5. (*be*) I *am* excited. 6. *(understand)* I *understand* your question. 7. *(appreciate)* I *appreciate* your time today.

Examples of Nonprogressive Verbs

Mental:				
know	*suppose*	*imagine*	*think*	*realize*
need	*understand*	*want*	*remember*	*prefer*
mean	*recognize*	*doubt*	*feel*	*believe*

Emotional:				
love	*dislike*	*mind*	*like*	*fear*
envy	*care*	*hate*	*appreciate*	

Possession:			
have	*possess*	*own*	*belong*

Sensory Perception:				
hear	*taste*	*smell*	*see*	*feel*

Other Actions:				
seem	*look*	*exist*	*owe*	*be*
contain	*cost*	*include*	*consist of*	*appear*
weigh				

He *realizes* the importance of in-store assembly.

3-2 Progressive / Action Verbs

Definition:	Examples:
Progressive or *action verbs* refer to or describe an action or activity in progress. *Note:* With progressive verbs, when describing a temporary characteristic, use (*be + adjective*). *Be* is most commonly used for foolish, nice, kind, lazy, careful, patient, silly, rude, polite and impolite actions. (**Example 5**)	**1.** (*feel*) She is *feeling* the soft, wool sweater. **2.** (*think*) Tim is *thinking* about studying at the library. **3.** (*taste*) My mom *tastes* the sauce. **4.** (*smell*) She *smells* the corn to check for freshness. **5.** (*be*) The clown is *being* silly. **6.** (*understanding*) I am not *understanding* the game. **7.** (*appreciating*) They are *appreciating* the help you gave them.

Exercise

Exercise 1: Choose whether the sentence is *progressive* or *nonprogressive*.

1. I *appreciate* the kind things you have done for me. <u>nonprogressive</u>

2. I *taste* the soup to make sure it is done. _____

3. She *is thinking* of a good present to get her brother. _____

4. The little girl *is looking* for her lost dog. _____

5. The butcher *is weighing* the meat to decide the price I must pay. _____

6. I *am sad* the little girl lost her dog. _____

7. Tom *appears* to be studying. _____

8. Seth *is smelling* the barbecue from inside the restaurant. _____

9. He *is seeing* too many patients. _____

10. Madeline *loves* to go out with her friends. _____

11. I *fear* roller coasters. _____

12. Mike *has* a beautiful car. _____

13. I *am thinking* about going to the theater. _____

14. John *is being* silly. _____

15. He *is having* car trouble. _____

16. He *wants* to be better at sports. _____

17. She *smells* good. _____

18. I truly *appreciate* your kindness. _____

19. I *remember* my sister's birthday every year. _____

20. The comedian *is appearing* at the club for one night only. _____

3-3 Using Expressions of Place with Progressive Tenses

Rule:	Examples:
You will often see an expression of place after the auxiliary verb *be* and the main verb ending with *-ing*. An expression of place always starts with a preposition.	**1.** Mike *is playing* at the playground. **2.** Seth *is sleeping* on the couch. **3.** Eric *was studying* at his desk. **4.** Emily *was reading* on the porch.

Sentence Structure Formula for *Expressions of Place*:

subject + ***verb/verb phrase*** + *prepositional phrase.*

1. It *is raining* in Seattle.
2. A baby *is crying* on my shoulder.
3. Birds *fly* in the sky.

Exercise

Exercise 1: Answer each question using the *expression of place*. The location of the *subject* is in parenthesis.

1. Question: Where is mom? *(work / in / office)*

   Answer: <u>Mom is working in her office.</u>

2. Question: Where is Mike? *(relax / at / home)*

   Answer: _____

3. Question: Where is Dad ? *(drive / to / store)*

   Answer: _____

4. Question: Is Jenny here? *(sleep / in / bedroom)*

   Answer: _____

5. Question: Where are you going for vacation? *(travel / to / California)*

   Answer: _____

6. Question: Where is Tom going? *(leave / for / airport)*

   Answer: _____

7. Question: Where is the cat? *(hide / under / bed)*

   Answer: _____

8. Question: Where is that great smell? *(come / from / kitchen)*

   Answer: _____

9. Question: Where is the dog? *(play / underneath / table)*

   Answer: _____

10. Question: Why is Jan leaving? *(move / to / New York)*

    Answer: _____

11. Question: Where is Mike? *(go / to / bookstore)*

    Answer: _____

3-4 Using the Present Progressive with Always

Rules:	Examples:
When explaining everyday or continuous actions, the word *always* is used. When using *always,* the sentences are referring to present time, and usually simple present is used. (**Example 1**)	**1.** I *always* go to the library every day after school.
English speakers may use *always* with the present progressive to complain, or to show annoyance or anger towards something or someone. (**Example 2**)	**2.** My son is *always* getting in trouble.
Furthermore, *forever* and *constantly* are also used with present progressive to show annoyance or anger towards something or someone. (**Example 3**)	**3.** He is *always/constantly* getting in trouble.

*Statement of Fact vs. Opinion:

1. Statement of fact: My son *always* gets in trouble.

2. Opinion: My son is *always* getting in trouble.

The boy *assumed* the balloons were for him.

Exercise

Exercise 1: Pretend your friend Michael has just bought a dog. Michael is stating problems that are wrong with his dog. Write Michael's complaints using the *present progressive* with *always*.

1. She barks loudly. *(always)* →

   Answer: <u>She's always barking loudly.</u>

2. She breaks my things. *(constantly)*

   Answer: _____

3. She makes me angry. *(forever)*

   Answer: _____

4. She steals food. *(constantly)*

   Answer: _____

5. She brings dead birds in the house. *(always)*

   Answer: _____

6. She chews on my shoes. *(constantly)*

   Answer: _____

7. She eats everything. *(always)*

   Answer: _____

8. She fights with other dogs. *(always)*

   Answer: _____

9. She runs away. *(always)*

   Answer: _____

10. She bites people. *(constantly)*

    Answer: _____

11. She scratches the furniture. *(always)*

    Answer: _____

Chapter 4
Transitive and Intransitive Verbs

Babies *cry.*

4-1 Intransitive Verbs

Definition:	Examples:
Verbs that are not followed by an object are called *intransitive verbs*.	**1.** Babies*(subject)* cry*(verb)*. **2.** Students*(subject)* read*(verb)*. **3.** People*(subject)* talk*(verb)*. **4.** Birds*(subject)* chirp*(verb)*. ***Note:*** there is no action going toward the object. There are no words following the verbs.

Common Intransitive Verbs:

agree	*arrive*	*come*	*cry*	*exist*
go	*happen*	*live*	*occur*	*rise*

Exercise

sing	compete	swim	bark	growl
learn	chirp	paint	cry	grow

Exercise 1: Match the words from the box with the words in the exercise below. Choose the answer choices that make the most sense.

1. Lions _growl_.

2. Birds _____.

3. Athletes _____.

4. Babies _____.

5. Plants _____.

6. Dogs _____.

7. Students _____.

8. Fish _____.

9. Musicians _____.

10. Artists _____.

4-2 Transitive Verbs

Definition:	Examples:
Verbs that are followed by an object are called *transitive verbs*.	1. The rain*(subject)* fell*(verb)* on the house*(object)*.
	2. The baby*(subject)* cried*(verb)* on my shoulder*(noun/object)*.
	3. The bird*(noun)* flew*(verb)* into the window*(noun/object)*.
	Note: there is an action going towards (→) the object.

Exercise

Exercise 1: Pick the correct answer choice by writing either *transitive* or *intransitive*.

1. A brother and his sister are yelling. _intransitive_

2. Babies like to cry. _____

3. That baby is crying so loudly. _____

4. She walked around the corner. _____

5. She walks quickly. _____

6. The birds flew. _____

7. The birds flew south for the winter. _____

8. She read loudly to the class. _____

9. She tested poorly. _____

10. He's concentrating. _____

11. The painter painted on the canvas. _____

12. She looked through the window. _____

13. Tom talks too loudly. _____

14. The car stopped. _____

15. The car stopped at the stop sign. _____

Chapter 5
Subject / Verb Agreement

He is **going to need a doctor.**

5-1 Subject / Verb Agreement

Rules:	Examples:
He / She / It are singular nouns, so you must use a singular verb. (**Example 1**)	1. He *is* going to the store.
is = singular auxiliary verb (**Example 2**)	2. She *is* going to the store.
He / She / It is (**Example 3**)	3. It *is* going to the store.
He / She / It bike*s*. (**Example 4**)	4. She runs all day. (***Note:*** You need an *-s* at the end of run.)
Note: *-s* is used at the end of the verb if the sentence has *He / She / It* as the subject.	***Note: Was*** can also be used as the past tense form of *is*.
They / You, use plural verbs (**Example 1**)	1. They *are* going to the store.
are = plural auxiliary verb (**Example 2**)	2. You *are* going to the store.
They / You / We are (**Example 3**)	3. They *are* looking at a car.
They / You / We run every day. (**Example 4**)	4. We *run* every day. (***Note:*** You do not need an *-s* at the end of run.)
Note: *-s* is <u>not</u> used at the end of the verb if the sentence has *They / You / We* as the subject.	*Note: **Were*** can also be used as the past tense form of *are*.

Continued

Rules:	Examples:
If the subject is a proper noun, you need an **-s** at the end of the verb or you need to use **is**, the auxiliary singular verb. (**Examples 1 and 2**)	**1.** The Statue of Liberty need**s** to be cleaned. **2.** The Statue of Liberty **is** green.

Exercise

Exercise 1: Choose the correct verb by writing the corresponding letter in the blank.

1. She _is_ running.
   a) is
   b) are

2. It _____ like rain.
   a) look
   b) looks

3. They_____ eating dinner.
   a) is
   b) are

4. My computer _____ black.
   a) is
   b) are

5. My teacher_____ nice.
   a) is
   b) are

6. You _____ to take a shower.
   a) need
   b) needs

7. The bus _____ on time.
   a) is
   b) are

8. The taxi drivers _____ driving fast.
   a) is
   b) are

9. He _____ to eat a lot.
    a) like
    b) likes

10. She _____ late.
    a) is
    b) are

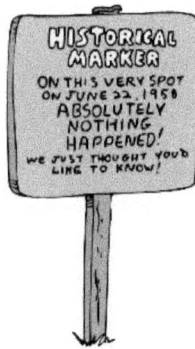

His time *and* money were wasted.

5-2 Subject / Verb Agreement Continued

Rules:	Examples:
When you have <u>two</u> or <u>more nouns</u> connected by ***and***, you must use a plural auxiliary verb.	**1.** Mike ***and*** Tom ***are*** at the movies. **2.** Emma ***and*** Sophia ***are*** best friends.
Use a singular auxiliary verb when you have <u>two</u> or <u>more singular nouns</u> or <u>pronouns</u> connected by ***or*** or ***nor***.	**1.** Mike ***nor*** Tom is ***going*** camping this week. **2.** ***Is*** the dog ***or*** cat visiting the veterinarian?
When a compound subject has <u>both a singular</u> and a <u>plural noun</u> or <u>pronoun</u> connected by ***or*** or ***nor***, the verb should agree with the part of the subject that is closest to the verb.	**1.** Mike or his ***friends*** ***are*** responsible for the accident. **2.** Mike or ***Tom*** ***is*** going to the store. **3.** ***Mike*** and ***Tom*** ***are*** going to the store.

Continued

Rules:	Examples:

Doesn't is a contraction of ***does not*** and should be used only with a singular subject.
 	
When you have the auxiliary verb ***does***:
 	
      he
 	
      she + ***doesn't***
 	
      it
 	
      John
	1. <u>***He doesn't***</u> want to go to the store.
	
	2. <u>***She doesn't***</u> like traveling.
	
	3. <u>***It doesn't***</u> snow in July.
	
	4. <u>***Mary doesn't***</u> like cold weather.

Don't is a contraction of ***do not*** and should be used with ***I***, ***they***, ***you***, ***we***, as well as proper and common noun subjects.
 	
When you have the auxiliary verb ***do***:
 	
      I
 	
      they
 	
      you + ***don't***
 	
      we
 	
      John and I
	1. <u>***They don't***</u> want to go to the store.
	
	2. <u>***I don't***</u> want to go to the store.
	
	3. <u>***You don't***</u> want to go to the store.
	
	4. <u>***We don't***</u> like hot weather.
	
	5. <u>***Peter and I***</u> **don't** go running at night.

Words like ***each***, ***each one***, ***either***, ***neither***, ***everyone***, ***everybody***, ***anybody***, ***anyone***, ***nobody***, ***somebody***, ***someone***, and ***no one*** are singular and require a singular verb.	**1.** <u>***Someone is***</u> going to the party. **2.** <u>***Everybody is***</u> looking for the boy. **3.** <u>***Nobody is***</u> running the race.

Exercise

Exercise 1: Underline the correct *verb* for each sentence.

    1. Josh and Tim *(is / <u>are</u>)* friends.

    2. Mike and six other people *(is / are)* at school today.

    3. John and four other people *(don't / doesn't)* want to take the bus.

4. The cat or dog *(were / was)* in the trash.

5. Mom and dad *(were / was)* yelling at the man.

6. She *(don't / doesn't)* want to go to the party.

7. He *(don't / doesn't)* want to go shopping.

8. It *(don't / doesn't)* look like it will rain.

9. Everyone *(is / are)* going to the park.

10. Somebody *(is / are)* in trouble.

11. Mike and I *(don't / doesn't)* want to go to Texas; we want to go to New York.

12. Jim and Sandy *(is / are)* getting married.

13. Nobody *(is / are)* going to the party at 8:00 p.m.

14. Each one *(is / are)* a different size.

15. My friends *(is / are)* traveling to Washington, D.C. for the July 4th parade.

Exercise 2: Determine whether the bold-printed verb in each sentence uses the correct verb form. If correct, write *correct*. If incorrect, rewrite the sentence with the correct form of the verb.

1. Carla **drove** to your house.

   correct

2. Jason and Elizabeth **rides** their bikes every day.

   _____

3. Michelle **teach** kindergarten.

   _____

4. Greg **live** in California.

   _____

5. Kari or Allison **has** the spare key.

   _____

6. The only way to pass tests *are* to study.

   _____

7. I *wants* to play football this season.

   _____

8. Ohio and Pennsylvania *are* next to each other.

   _____

9. The flowers you bought me *is* lovely.

   _____

10. Every Thanksgiving, David and Maria *makes* pumpkin pie.

    _____

11. Karen *needs* to borrow your car.

    _____

12. She *make* coffee.

    _____

5-3 Subject / Verb Agreement with Count / Noncount Nouns

Rules:	Examples:
Noncount nouns are singular and need a singular verb.	1. The **_water_ _is_** good. 2. The **_coffee_ _tastes_** great. 3. The **_soda_ _looks_** like Coke.
Count nouns can be both singular and plural. The verb needs to match the subject of the sentence.	1. The **_books_ _are_** on the table. 2. The **_book_ _is_** on the table.
Collective nouns are nouns that mean more than one person. Collective nouns are used with singular verbs. (**Examples:** *team*, *group*, *party*)	1. The **_team_ _won_** the competition. 2. We **_made_** a reservation for a **party** of five.

The mystery *spot is* truly a mystery.

Exercise

Exercise 1: Follow the rules of *subject/verb agreement* with *count/noncount nouns*, and choose the correct word for each sentence.

1. Seth and Beth *are* (is/are) married.

2. Mike and Ben _____ *(look / looks)* happy.

3. Mike and his dogs _____ *(is / are)* taking a walk.

4. Mike or his friend _____ *(is / are)* looking for the dog.

5. He _____ *(don't / doesn't)* want to go to the store.

6. They _____ *(don't / doesn't)* like traveling by car.

7. Someone _____ *(is / are)* looking for the child's parents.

8. The weather _____ *(is / are)* looking good.

9. The computers _____ *(is / are)* broken.

10. The club _____ *(is / are)* difficult to get into.

Chapter 6
Adjectives and Adverbs

Fixing a toilet is not the *easiest* of tasks.

6-1 Adjectives

Adjectives modify or describe nouns. The adjective's job is to give more information about the noun or pronoun.

Rules:	Examples:	Sample Sentences:
An adjective cannot be singular or plural. The letter *–s* is never added to the end of an adjective.	*beautiful* *friendly* *stupid* *weird* *hungry* *tired* *hot* *shy* *lazy* *bad*	**Correct:** He is a *bad* driver. **Incorrect:** He is a *bads* driver. **Correct:** It looks *cold* outside. **Incorrect:** It looks *colds* outside.

Exercise

important	helpful	few	tallest	boiling
careful	embarrassed	best	shallow	angry

Exercise 1: Fill in each blank with an adjective that makes sense.

1. When I asked Jessica for assistance, she was not very _helpful_.

2. I was so _____ when my dad started singing at the grocery store!

3. Matt is the _____ boy in the entire school.

4. It is _____ to read all of the instructions before beginning the assignment.

5. _____ people can recite the entire Preamble of the Constitution.

6. Once the water is _____, you can add the spaghetti.

7. Sheila is better is than I am at playing the piano, but I think Mary is _____.

8. Since I can't swim, I stay in the _____ end of the pool.

9. I am _____ that I wasn't invited to the party.

10. Be _____ what you wish for.

6-2 Adverbs

Adverbs modify or describe verbs, and often answer the question of <u>how</u>.

Rules:	Examples:	Sample Sentences:
You can often add *–ly* to the end of an adjective to make an adverb.	**Adjectives** *slow* *extreme* *rapid* *quick* **Adverbs** *slowly* *extremely* *rapidly* *quickly*	**Question:** Is gas expensive? **Answer:** Yes, it's ***extremely*** expensive. **Question:** How fast does she run? **Answer:** She runs ***very quickly***. I am ***rapidly*** completing my homework.
Adverbs are also used to state the time or frequency an action is occurring.	*always* *never* *sometimes* *soon* *today* *tomorrow* *yesterday*	**1.** I will go back to school ***tomorrow***. **2.** I will ***never*** run a marathon.
Some adverbs occur in the middle of a sentence. These adverbs can: come in front of simple present and simple past words. (except *be*). (**Example 1**) come after *be*. (**Example 2**) come between a helping verb and a main verb. (**Example 3**) come directly after the subject, when in a question form. (**Example 4**)	**Common Mid-Sentence Adverbs** *always* *already* *ever* *finally* *generally* *hardly* *ever* *just* *never* *not ever* *often* *probably* *rarely* *seldom* *sometimes* *usually*	**1.** He ***usually*** comes late. **2.** He is ***usually*** late. **3.** He has ***frequently*** come late. **4.** Does he ***usually*** come late?

Continued

Rules:	Examples:	Sample Sentences:
The word **well**	*well (adjective)*	**1.** My grandfather's health is decreasing and he is not **well**. **2.** The instructor teaches **well**. **well = good*

He is *finally* having fun at his job.

Exercise

Exercise 1: Use an *adverb* from the box below to best complete each sentence. Each *adverb* is only used once.

daily	clumsily	famously	jokingly	poorly	slowly
softly	tearfully	wisely	vaguely	unlikely	yesterday

1. It is <u>unlikely</u> that I will finish my homework before dinner.

2. _____ I told my aunt I'd babysit for her. Now I don't want to.

3. Brush your teeth twice _____.

4. This is where Dr. Martin Luther King, Jr. _____ delivered his "I Have a Dream" speech.

5. She _____ remembers what the thief looked like.

6. It is hard to hear Karen because she speaks so _____.

7. After spinning around in circles, we _____ fell down laughing.

8. When I _____ told Amy that I didn't like her haircut, she cried.

9. When my sister left for college, we _____ hugged and said goodbye.

10. After coming face to face with a snake, I backed away _____, even though I wanted to run.

11. Carla _____ chose the correct answer and won a million dollars!

12. After doing _____ on the test, I asked Mrs. Peters for help after school.

Exercise 2: Write the correct *adverb* or *adjective* in each sentence.

1. She drives slowly *(slow, slowly)*.

2. My mom is a _____ *(slow, slowly)* driver.

3. I mow my lawn _____ *(frequent, frequently)*.

4. She is a _____ *(quick, quickly)* walker.

5. She walked to the store _____ *(quick, quickly)*.

6. I am _____ *(rare, rarely)* on that side of town.

7. You must enter the movie theater _____ *(quiet, quietly)*.

8. She does her work _____ *(poor, poorly)*.

9. She is a _____ *(poor, poorly)* student.

10. They dug _____ *(deep, deeply)* into the ground.

11. She drew a _____ *(beautiful, beautifully)* portrait.

12. She drew the portrait _____ *(beautiful, beautifully)*.

6-3 Adjective Clauses

An *adjective clause* is used to describe the noun in a sentence.

Clause:	Rules:	Examples:
Who	**Who** is used for humans and domestic animals. Use **who** when your subject is followed by an auxiliary verb or an adverb. ***Note:*** Domestic animals are animals, humans use for pets. (Ex: dogs, cats, birds, etc)	My friend, **who** <u>is</u> the nicest person in the world, gave me a great birthday present. (**who = my friend**)
		My dog, **who** <u>always</u> gets in trouble, needed to go to the veterinarian today. ***Note:*** The subject is followed by an adverb.
Whom	**Whom** is used for humans. Use **whom** when your subject is followed by a noun or a possessive adjective. ***Note:*** See page 94 for a list of possessive adjectives.	Dr. Crew, **whom** <u>Ben</u> doesn't like, is my teacher in math class. (**whom = Dr. Crew**)
Which	**Which** is used for things and animals.	Seth has a book **which** has great pictures. (**which = book**)
That	**That** is used for humans, animals or things.	John is writing a paper **that** his professor assigned. (**that = paper**)
Where	**Where** is used to represent a location.	The apartment **where** I live is in a good location. (**where = apartment**)
When	**When** is used to represent a specific time.	That time **when** I broke my arm was horrible. (**when = time**)
Whose	**Whose** is used to show ownership.	I know the girl **whose** essay won an award. (**whose = girl**)

Exercise

Exercise 1: Using the list above choose the correct *adjective clause* for each sentence.

1. Mike has a dog <u>that</u> chews many things. *(whose / when / that)*

2. I know a friend _____ mother is the president of a company. *(whose / that / when)*

3. I know a place _____ the chicken is outstanding. *(when / where / that)*

4. Dr. Linda, _____ my friend loves, is not accepting patients. *(that / when / whom)*

5. My cat _____ is the best cat in the world, loves mice. *(when / whose / who)*

6. The computer _____ I wanted to buy is too expensive. *(that / where / when)*

7. The police have not caught the person _____ hit my car yesterday. *(when / whose / who)*

8. The book _____ I borrowed from Linda has been stolen. *(when / where / that)*

9. That time _____ I lost my dog was very sad for me. *(when / where / that)*

10. The man _____ house I am looking to purchase is willing to lower the price. *(whose / that / when)*

Chapter 7
Contractions and Articles

He's **wishing he would have chosen another copier.**

7-1 Contractions

Contractions are made when nouns, pronouns or certain forms of *be* are combined with an auxiliary verb to make one word.

Common Contractions:	Examples:
1. I + am = ***I'm***	**1.** ***I'm*** traveling this summer.
2. it + is = ***it's***	**2.** ***It's*** my birthday.
3. is + not = ***isn't***	**3.** She ***isn't*** going.
4. it + has = ***it's***	**4.** ***It's*** been a very long time.
5. they + have = ***they've***	**5.** ***They've*** gone to the movies.
6. she/he/(etc.) + would = ***she'd/he'd***	**6.** ***She'd*** want you to have these pictures.
7. I/she/he/(etc.) + will = ***I'll/she'll/he'll***	**7.** ***I'll*** go to the store and get some bread.

Continued

Common Contractions:	Examples:
8. you + are = ***you're***	**8.** ***You're*** very wet.
9. will + not = ***won't***	**9.** I ***won't*** be cold if I wear a sweater.

Exercise

Exercise 1: Complete each *contraction*.

1. could + not = <u>couldn't</u>

2. _____ + would = she'd

3. _____ + am = I'm

4. _____ + not = hadn't

5. might + have = _____

6. it + _____ = It'll

7. will + not = _____

8. _____ + are = we're

9. _____ + will = you'll

10. what + have = _____

11. Do + _____ = don't

Exercise 2: Change each word phrase into a *contraction*.

1. *(It is)* <u>It's</u> for sale.

2. *(I am)* _____ a student.

3. The car *(is not)* _____ for sale.

4. *(I will)* _____ go to the store.

5. *(It has)* _____ been great.

6. *(They have)* _____ gone to the store.

7. *(You are)* _____ out of pretzels. *(The word "out" means: there is "0" left.)*

8. *(We are)* _____ out of time.

9. *(We will)* _____ be back at 5:00pm.

10. *(She would)* _____ go to the store if she had a car.

7-2 Articles

Article:	Rules:	Examples:
The	*The* is used in front of the noun of the sentence. *The* is specific. When using *the*, you are using an exact subject. *The* is not general.	1. *The* dog is eating. 2. *The* Statue of Liberty is green.
A	*A* is used in front of the noun in the sentence. *A* is general. *A* means everyone or everything, not just a specific person or thing.	1. *A* dog has four legs. 2. *A* man has *a* nose.
Noncount Nouns	When noncount nouns are the subject of the sentence, and they are saying a generalization (not specific), do not use *the* or *a* in front of the noun.	**Incorrect:** ~~The~~ apples are red. **Correct:** Apples are red.
***The* and Noncount Nouns**	If you are being <u>specific</u>, then use *the* in front of the noun.	**Incorrect:** Apples are red. **Correct:** *The* apples are red.

Continued

Article:	Rules:	Examples:
A/An	If the first letter of the noun starts with a vowel, use *an*. If the first letter of the noun starts with a consonant use *a*.	1. *An* apple 2. *An* office 3. *A* desk 4. *A* book

Helpful Tip:

It is always important to tell the listener or reader <u>how many</u> of the noun, you mean.	1. *An* Apple 2. Apple*(s)* 3. *Several* apples 4. *A* few apples 5. *The* apple

The smoke is not a good sign.

Exercise

Exercise 1: Choose the correct *article* for each sentence.

1. Question: Do you have <u>the</u> homework I assigned yesterday?

   Answer: Yes, I do.

2. Question: Do you have _____ pencil?

   Answer: Yes, I do.

3. Question: Do you have _____ idea?

   Answer: Yes, I absolutely do.

4. Question: Do you have _____ soda?

   Answer: Yes, we do.

5. Question: Do you have _____ dog?

   Answer: Yes, I do.

6. Question: Does she work in _____ office?

   Answer: Yes, she does.

7. Question: Is he _____ orphan?

   Answer: No, he isn't.

8. Question: Do you have _____ pencil?

   Answer: No, I don't have pencil.

9. Question: Do you have _____ book you borrowed?

   Answer: Yes, I have the book.

10. Question: Can I use _____ computer?

    Answer: Yes, you can use computer.

11. Question: Can I have _____ money you owe me?

    Answer: Yes, you can.

Chapter 8
The Tenses

He *learns* to fly.

8-1 The Simple Tenses

Rules:	Examples:
Simple present expresses events or situations that exist always, usually or habitually; they exist now, they existed in the past, and they probably will exist in the future. (**Examples: 1 and 2**)	**1.** It *rains* <u>in Seattle</u>. **2.** I *exercise* <u>every day</u>. **3.** It *rained* <u>yesterday</u>.
Simple past expresses a specific time in the past when the action happened. The action began and ended in the past. (**Examples: 3 and 4**)	**4.** It *rained* non-stop <u>last month</u>. **5.** It *will snow* <u>tomorrow</u>.
Simple future expresses a specific time in the future when the action will happen, but it has not started yet. (**Examples: 5 and 6**)	**6.** The forecast *predicts* snow <u>next week</u>.

Continued

Sentence Structure Formula:

Simple present:
subject + verb(simple present) + preposition + direct object
It **rains** in Seattle.

Simple past:
subject + verb(simple past) + adverb
It **rained** yesterday.

Simple future:
subject + auxiliary verb(simple future) + main verb(simple present) + adverb
It **will snow** tomorrow.

8-2 The Perfect Tenses

The *perfect tenses* all give the idea that a specific time or event happens before another specific time or event.

Rules:	Examples:	Explanations:
Present perfect states a certain time or event has happened in the past and the time or event is ending in the present.	He **has slept** for six hours.	They finished sleeping directly before the current time. The exact time may be unknown.
Past perfect states that a certain time or event has happened in the past and has finished in the past.	She had **already slept** <u>when they arrived</u>.	First, she finished sleeping. After she slept, they then arrived.
Future perfect states that a certain time or event will happen in the future and will finish in the future.	He **will already have slept** <u>when they arrive</u>.	First, she will finish sleeping. After she has slept, she will then arrive. She will finish sleeping before they arrive.

Note: Use **already** to explain that you will finish or have finished an action.

Continued

Sentence Structure Formula:

Present Perfect:
have/has + *past participle*
You **have** *watched* television for two hours; please turn it off.

Past Perfect:
had + *past participle*
When they arrived, the baby **had** already *gone* to sleep.

Future Perfect:
will have + *past participle*
I **will** already **have** *eaten* when I arrive.

8-3 The Perfect Progressive Tenses

The *perfect progressive* tenses say that an event is happening immediately before, up to, until another time or event. The tenses are used to express the length of time of the first event.

Rules:	Examples:	Explanations:
Present perfect progressive states the length of time an action has been happening up to the present time.	I **have been studying** for three hours.	He/she started studying in the past and has continued studying up to the present. ***How Long? For three hours.***
Past perfect progressive states the length of time an action happened in the past.	I **had been studying** for two hours before I stopped for lunch.	An event that had taken place in the past for a certain length of time, and ended before another event in the past.
Future perfect progressive states the length of time an action will happen in the future.	I **will have been studying** for two hours before they arrive.	An event that will happen in the future for a certain length of time and will end before another event in the future.

Continued

Sentence Structure Formula:

Present Perfect Progressive:
have + **been** + *(verb)-**ing** (present participle)*

Past Perfect Progressive:
had + **been** + *(verb)-**ing** (present participle)*

Future Perfect Progressive:
will have + **been** + *(verb)-**ing** (present participle)*

8-4 The Progressive Tenses

The *progressive tense* is used when there is an action in progress during a certain time. The action starts before, takes place during, and continues after a <u>different</u> time or action.

Rules:	Examples:	Explanations:
Present progressive describes an action that has happened in the past, it is currently happening in the present, and it will continue in the future. The actual time or date the action will stop is unknown.	It *is raining* right now.	It was raining in the past. It is now currently raining in the present, and the rain will continue in the future. The actual time or date the rain will stop is unknown.
Past progressive describes an action that has started at a certain time in the past. It is possible for the action to be currently happening now. It is also possible for the action to continue in the future.	It *was raining* when I arrived.	It was raining in the past. It may be raining now. It may continue to rain the future.
Future progressive describes an action that will begin in the future and will continue to a certain time in the future.	It *will be raining* when we arrive.	It will in rain the future, and the rain will continue at a certain time in the future.

Continued

Sentence Structure Formula:

Present progressive:
be + *(verb)-**ing***
The teacher *is talking* right now.

Past progressive:
be + *(verb)-**ing***
It *was snowing* when I got to my house.

Future progressive:
will be + *(verb)-**ing***
It *will be raining* when we arrive.

8-5 Using Expressions of Place with Progressive Tenses

Rules:	Examples:
Expressions of place with progressive tenses describes <u>where</u> the action is happening. A verb using present, past or future progressive will always be followed by a *statement of place*.	**1.** The man is ***hiding*** behind the clock. The man is ***hiding*** *(progressive)* <u>behind the clock.</u> *(statement of place)* **2.** John is ***running*** <u>on the street</u>. John is ***running*** *(progressive)* <u>on the street</u>. *(statement of place)* **3.** Mike is ***reading*** <u>in his room</u>. Mike is ***reading*** *(progressive)* ***in his room***. *(statement of place)*

Sentence Structure Formula:

Expressions of place with progressive tenses:
progressive + <u>statement of place</u>
Chris is *writing* <u>on his desk</u>.

He is *learning in flight school*.

Exercise

Exercise 1: Use either *simple present* or *present progressive* to change the words in parenthesis to the correct form.

1. Mike cannot come outside because he *(clean)* <u>is cleaning</u> his room.

2. Mike *(clean)* _____ his room every day.

3. Ashley *(sleep)* _____ right now. Can you come back later?

4. It *(rain)* _____ a lot in Seattle.

5. Seth *(run)* _____ every day after school.

6. It *(snow)* _____ in Ohio.

7. I *(watch)* _____ TV every day after school.

8. She *(run)* _____ errands each day between 2:00pm and 4:00pm.

9. It is *(hail)* _____ right now in Florida.

10. The volcano has lava *(flow)* _____ out of the top.

11. I *(bike)* _____ to work on Fridays.

Exercise 2: Use *past perfect* to change the words in parenthesis to the correct form.

1. I *(study)* <u>studied</u> the information before I took my driving test.

2. I *(clean)* _____ my room three days ago.

3. She *(sleep)* _____ for two hours before I came in and woke her up.

4. He *(look)* _____ at the material before he took the test.

5. My boss *(ask)* _____ me to work yesterday, so I cannot go to the mall today.

Exercise 3: Use *future progressive* to change the words in parenthesis to the correct form.

1. I *(work)* <u>will work</u> today, so come by and visit me.

2. I *(call)* _____ you after school.

3. I *(discuss)* _____ this with your father after school.

4. She *(study)* _____ all afternoon.

5. She *(talk)* _____ to the professor after class.

Chapter 9
Gerunds

He is scared of *skiing*.

9-1 Gerunds

Definition:	Examples:
A *gerund* is a noun made from a verb by adding **-ing**. The gerund form of the verb **read** is **reading**. You can use a gerund as the <u>subject</u>, the <u>complement</u>, or the <u>object</u> of a sentence.	1. ***Writing*** helps an English learner study English. *("**Writing**" is used as the subject of the sentence.)* 2. Tom's favorite activity is ***running***. *("**Running**" is complementing the sentence.)* 3. She loves ***skiing***. *("**Skiing**" is the object of the sentence.)*
A speaker can also write and speak gerunds in the <u>negative</u> by adding **not**.	1. She is <u>not</u> ***working*** at her job today. 2. Tom is <u>not</u> ***watching*** the game until noon.

Exercise

Exercise 1: Complete the sentence with the correct *gerund* form.

1. *(Run)* Running is my favorite exercise.

2. I love *(read)* _____.

3. *(Read)* _____ is a good way to learn English.

4. A good outdoor activity is *(bike)* _____.

5. *(Speak)* _____ is my favorite part about learning.

6. Tom's favorite activity is *(hike)* _____.

7. Bird *(watch)* _____ is my favorite activity.

8. *(Drive)* _____ is difficult for me.

9. *(Listen)* _____ to my mother speak is difficult.

10. *(Type)* _____ is the best way to write your school papers.

9-2 Gerunds that Come after Verbs

Rules:	Examples:
Use a *gerund after a verb* when a speaker is performing an action and the speaker wants the listener to know that the action is continuous.	1. She ***suggested going*** to a movie. 2. Mary ***keeps talking*** about her problems. 3. Tom ***loves sailing*** in the bay.

Exercise

Exercise 1: Underline the *gerund-phrase* combination in each sentence.

1. The author <u>liked writing</u> the book.

2. The musician enjoyed playing the instrument.

3. The athlete began running at noon.

4. The girl continued talking to her friend.

5. The student kept typing on her computer.

6. The mom started yelling at her child.

7. The teacher allowed talking in his class.

8. The artist stopped painting after he sold his artwork.

9. They liked going the store.

10. My mom keeps cleaning my room.

11. They enjoy traveling to the beach.

12. Mike likes listening to the professor.

13. Mary suggested running the marathon.

14. Ann likes participating in class.

15. The teacher likes giving us homework.

9-3 Gerunds Can Often Be Modified with Possessive Forms

Rules:	Examples:
Gerunds can often be modified with possessive and object pronouns.	1. The teacher warned John about *his* <u>yelling</u>. 2. The coach wanted *me* <u>practicing</u>.
Gerunds can also be modified by common and proper nouns.	1. The teacher complained about *Mike's* <u>yelling</u>. 2. Melissa loves *Stacy's* <u>cooking</u>.

The veterinarian warned him about Pete's *growing*.

Exercise

crafting	listening	singing	studying	working
resting	practicing	learning	praying	designing

Exercise 1: Using the box above, write the *gerund* that makes the most sense.

    1. The teacher wanted us <u>learning</u>.

    2. The coach needed her _____.

    3. The musician loved Gloria's _____.

    4. My best friend really appreciated me _____ to her problems.

    5. The furniture buyer worried about the carpenter _____ the wrong chair.

    6. I needed the student _____.

    7. I took the car to the mechanic and said, "I need the car _____."

    8. The doctor needed the patient _____.

    9. The priest wanted them _____.

  10. We needed the architect _____.

He likes to *go parasailing*.

9-4 *Go* + Gerund

Rules:	Examples:
When a speaker is describing his actions while performing an activity, use **go + gerund**. **Go + gerund** is used for all recreational activities. *Note:* the past tense of **go** is **went**.	**1.** I **go sailing** once a month. **2.** We **went sailing** last weekend.

Sample List of Go + Gerund

go boating	*go bowling*	*go camping*	*go dancing*
go fishing	*go hiking*	*go hunting*	*go jogging*
go sailing	*go shopping*	*go sightseeing*	*go skiing*
go swimming	*go sledding*	*go surfing*	*go driving*

She likes to *go rafting*.

Exercise

Exercise 1: Write the correct *go + gerund* form for each sentence.

1. I like to *(fish)* go fishing.

2. I *(walk)* _____ every day.

3. Tom *(run)* _____ in the afternoons.

4. Mary is *(exercise)* _____.

5. We are *(swim)* _____.

6. Ann is *(hike)* _____.

7. The students are *(study)* _____.

8. The mother *(jog)* _____ every day after work.

9. Tom *(smoke)* _____ every afternoon.

10. Lisa is *(shop)* _____.

Chapter 10
Infinitives

He is happy *to rake* leaves.

10-1 Infinitives

Definition:	Examples:
Infinitives are the *to* form of the verb. **Note:* you can also use an infinitive as the subject, the complement, or the object of a sentence. The infinitive form of *learn* is *to learn*.	**1. *To learn*** is important. *(subject of the sentence)* **2.** The most important thing is *to learn*. *(complement of the sentence)* **3.** He wants *to learn*. *(object of the sentence)*
Infinitives can also be made negative by adding *not*.	**1.** I decided *not to go*. **2.** The most important thing is *not to give up*.

Exercise

treat	play	paint	hike	perform
listen	write	design	treat	train

Exercise 1: Complete the sentence with the correct *infinitive* or *gerund* form.

1. The artist only likes <u>to paint</u>.

2. Tom loves the outdoors and his favorite activity is _____.

3. When I go to class, my teacher always tells me _____.

4. The architect loves _____.

5. The baseball player wants _____.

6. The doctor has chosen _____ his patient.

7. The author likes _____ in the evening.

8. The singer refuses _____ for small crowds.

9. I do not understand why my computer refuses _____.

10. I cannot get my mp3 _____.

10-2 A Verb Followed by an Infinitive

Rule:	Examples:
Use an *infinitive after a verb* when a speaker is performing an action, and the speaker wants or needs to perform another action immediately after the first action.	**1.** She ***wants to go*** to a movie. **2.** Mary ***needs to talk*** about her problems. **3.** Tom ***likes to read*** fiction.

Sentence Structure Formula:

verb + preposition + verb(infinitive)
She ***has to leave*** before noon.

Exercise

afford	agreed	fail	begin	care
happen	forget	need	needs	attempt

Exercise 1: Choose the correct *verb* from the box above. Then change the *verb* to an *infinitive* to complete the sentence.

1. My dad <u>needs</u> to ask for directions.

2. Why did you _____ to tell me that I needed to bring my swimsuit?

3. I _____ to start studying as soon as the movie is over.

4. I don't _____ to hold your pet snake.

5. I _____ to make three dozen cookies for the party.

6. Don't _____ to brush your teeth!

7. I _____ to know the owner of the restaurant.

8. Let's _____ to answer your questions.

9. I can't _____ to understand what you are going through.

10. Maria can't _____ to fail another Biology test.

10-3 A Verb Followed by a Noun + an Infinitive

Rule:	Examples:
Use a *verb followed by a noun + infinitive* when a person/animal wants another person/animal to do a specific action. *Note:* a pronoun can come before the noun.	**1.** The teacher <u>wanted her students</u> ***to speak***. **2.** Mike <u>asked Tom</u> ***to leave***. **3.** The dog <u>wants you</u> ***to give*** him a treat.

Sentence Structure Formula:

verb + noun + verb(infinitive)
Susan ***asked Richard to donate*** money.

Exercise

to practice	to dig	to sing	to learn	to deposit

Exercise 1:Using the phrases in the box. Complete each sentence with the correct *infinitive* form.

1. The coach wanted his athletes <u>to practice</u>.

2. My teacher wanted me _____.

3. The banker wanted me _____, not withdrawal.

4. The gardener wanted me _____.

5. The music teacher wanted me _____.

He *wanted his friend to move* faster.

10-4 An Adjective Followed by an Infinitive

Rule:	Examples:
Use an *adjective followed by an infinitive* in order to express the way they feel about a certain action.	**1**. She is ***quick to move***.
	2. Seth is ***slow to learn***.
	3. She is ***scarred to go*** alone.

Sentence Structure Formula:

adjective + infinitive
Tom is ***happy to invite*** Susan

Exercise

Exercise 1: You are Christopher Columbus and your crew is ready to turn the ships around and head back home. The sentences below are things you may say to your crew to keep them motivated. Underline the *noun* and *infinitive* phrases in each sentence below.

1. Every <u>attempt to</u> turn the ship around has failed.

2. Don't you understand that I have a need to see the rest of the world?

3. The king and queen have granted permission to explore.

4. It is my wish to see land.

5. There is a way to get around the world that we haven't seen yet!

6. This is a reminder to always dream!

7. I have a goal to explore every inch of this world.

8. I have a plan to find gold and other riches.

9. It is my decision to keep sailing. We will reach land soon!

10. If there is any refusal to keep sailing, we will throw you overboard!

10-5 *Be* Followed by an Adjective + an Infinitive

Rule:	Examples:
Use *be followed by an adjective + an infinitive* in order to describe their emotion towards a direct action.	**1.** He *is glad to be* done.
	2. They *were good to go*.
	3. She *was quick to act*.

Sentence Structure Formula:

be + adjective + infinitive
Susan *is excited to move*.

Exercise

Exercise 1: Underline the *be+adjective+infinitive* combinations in the paragraph below. There are ten.

It's going to <u>be sad to</u> move away from my hometown, but my mom said I should realize how great it is to go to a new city. "Other kids would be fortunate to have a new city with new friends!" is what she keeps telling me. "You'd be amazed to see how many friends I already have here," is what I keep telling her. I'll be certain to keep in touch with everyone though. I guess I should be grateful to at least go to a city that is on the beach. My older sister is really excited. She thinks our hometown is so boring, but I think she should be proud to live here! She doesn't think I should be scared to move, but I love my house, and I love my friends! I'll be sorry to leave everything behind! I guess I have to be willing to try something new. She said I will be relieved to know that my new school is in walking distance to our new house. I guess that makes me feel a little better.

10-6 *Too* Followed by an Adjective / Adverb + Infinitive

Rule:	Examples:
Use *too followed by an adjective/adverb + infinitive* in order to express the exaggeration of an action.	**1.** It is *too windy to drive*.
	2. They talk *too loudly to study*.
	3. You are *too late to take* the test.

Sentence Structure Formula:

too + adjective/adverb + infinitive
Tom is *too afraid to fly*.

Exercise

Exercise 1: Rewrite each sentence placing the word *too* in the correct place. Then, complete the sentence with the correct *infinitive*.

1. The car is old. *(drive)*

   <u>The car is too old to drive.</u>

2. The light is dim. *(see)*

   _____

3. The music loud. *(study)*

   _____

4. The computer is expensive. *(purchase)*

   _____

5. The box is heavy. *(move)*

   _____

6. It is hot. *(run)*

   _____

7. The bridge is icy. *(cross)*

   _____

8. The library is quiet. *(talk)*

   _____

9. The pool is shallow. *(dive)*

   _____

10. They are excited. *(sleep)*

    _____

11. The company is big. *(fail)*

    _____

Exercise Continued

to make mistakes.	to have a conversation.	to not wear a jacket.	to speak in public.
to go swimming.	to run a race.	to wear sunglasses.	to type my paper.
to pay his bills.	to read in one day.	to eat another bite.	

Exercise 2: The word *too* has been taken out of all of the sentences. Rewrite each sentence placing the word *too* in the correct place in each sentence. Then, finish each sentence using one of the phrases from the box above.

1. The music is loud.

   The music is too loud to have a conversation.

2. It's cold outside.

   _____

3. The water is cold.

   _____

4. She is slow.

_____

5. The book is long.

_____

6. David is full.

_____

7. Mike is poor.

_____

8. Jessica is careful.

_____

9. The sky is dark.

_____

10. Arthur is nervous.

_____

11. The computer is broken.

_____

They sing *too loudly to hear* anyone else.

10-7 *Enough* followed by a Noun(s) + Infinitive

Rule:	Examples:
Use *enough followed by a noun(s) + infinitive* in order to express the maximum completion of a specific action. **Enough** states that the speaker has done all of the action and cannot do anymore, or chooses not to do anymore.	**1.** Tom applied for **enough scholarships to pay** for school. **2.** John earned **enough money to pay** for his trip. **3.** Jake bought **enough wood to start** a fire.

Sentence Structure Formula:

enough + noun(s) + infinitive
Gloria does not have **enough apples to make** the pie.

Exercise

Exercise 1: The word *enough* has been taken out of all of the sentences. Rewrite each sentence placing the word *enough* in the correct place in each sentence.

1. She doesn't have money to go to the movies.

   <u>She doesn't have enough money to go to the movies.</u>

2. Tom has money to buy his bike.

   _____

3. You must drink to hydrate yourself.

   _____

4. They must practice English to speak well.

   _____

5. She did not run fast to win the marathon race.

   _____

6. Tom did not swim quick to win the meet.

   _____

7. The joke was not funny to laugh.

   _____

8. The water was not warm to take a shower.

   _____

9. They did not read to take the test.

   _____

10. She did not talk to receive the job.

   _____

Chapter 11
Personal Pronouns (Part 1)

She had too much wine.

11-1 Personal Pronouns

Pronouns are nouns used to replace a noun in a sentence. In American English, pronouns are used so you do not need to continue using the same noun many times in a sentence or conversation. The noun that the pronoun is referring to is called an *antecedent*.

Note: pronouns are also used if the speaker or writer does not know the exact name of a person, place, thing, or idea but the speaker or writer wants to talk about it.

Subject Pronouns	Singular	Plural	Sample Sentences:
	I *you* *he, she, it*	*we* *you* *they*	I rode the ***roller coaster***. **It** was fast. ***Roller Coaster** = antecedent * *it* = pronoun
			Question: Where did Mike and Tom go? **Answer:** *They* went to the carnival. ***Mike and Tom** = antecedent ***They** = pronoun

Object Pronouns	Singular	Plural	Sample Sentences:
	me *you* *him, her* *it*	*us* *you, them*	"Mike, ***you*** should do your homework. ***You*** are going to fail the test tomorrow."

Exercise

Exercise 1: Identify the *antecedent* and the *pronoun* in each sentence.

1. The game was great. It was the best I had ever seen.
   antecedent = <u>game</u> / pronoun = <u>It</u>

2. I enjoyed going to the zoo and looking at the gorillas. They are large animals.

   antecedent = _____ / pronoun = _____

3. My mother made me steak last night. She cooked it perfectly.

   antecedent = _____ / pronoun = _____

4. I can't find the remote anywhere. Where could it be?

   antecedent = _____ / pronoun = _____

5. The potato chips where delicious. They had the perfect amount of salt.

   antecedent = _____ / pronoun = _____

6. We went to see the Statue of Liberty last year. I didn't know how large it was.

   antecedent = _____ / pronoun = _____

7. The young man was accepted into the university. He was very excited.

   antecedent = _____ / pronoun = _____

8. The light bulb blew out. It did not last very long. (blew out = stopped working)

   antecedent = _____ / pronoun = _____

9. Having two older brothers is great. They always protect me.

   antecedent = _____ / pronoun = _____

10. My grandfather is a great man. He gives me a lot of knowledge and wisdom.

    antecedent = _____ / pronoun = _____

11-2 Subject Pronouns

Definition:	Subject Pronouns:	Examples:
The subject is the person, place, place, thing or idea that's doing the action. *Subject pronouns* are simply subjects put in pronoun form.	*I* *you* *he* *she* *it* *we* *they*	*He* likes running on the street. *He* is the subject/pronoun. *Likes* is the verb. *Street* is the object.

Exercise

Exercise 1: Rewrite the following sentences using *personal pronouns* as the *subject*.

1. John was waiting for the rain to stop.

   He was waiting for the rain to stop.

2. Elizabeth has never seen the movie.

   _____

3. Lewis and Clark explored America.

   _____

4. Jason made everyone dinner.

   _____

5. The remote was under a sofa cushion.

   _____

6. My dentist told me that I didn't need braces. I didn't believe him.

   _____

Exercise 2: In the sentences below, fill in the blank with the correct *subject pronouns*.

1. Kelly wants to go shopping. <u>She</u> needs new shoes.

2. David likes riding his bike around town. _____ says it's the best form of exercise.

3. Jessica and I don't agree on everything, but _____ do agree on what movie to see.

4. Mrs. Richards graded our tests. _____ said we all passed.

5. Greg and Linda missed recess today. _____ had to make up a test.

6. If Missy doesn't tell us what kind of ice cream to buy, _____ will have to eat vanilla.

7. The cat is happily sleeping. _____ only wakes up for meals.

8. The play takes place in Pittsburgh. _____ is based on a true story.

9. Debbie and Heather are working hard. _____ are always competing with each other.

10. The coach said that I need to practice more. _____ thinks I could be a lot faster.

11. The musicians are trying to sell their CD. _____ think it will make them rich!

11-3 Object Pronouns

Definition:	Object Pronouns:	Examples:
The object is the person, place, thing or idea that is receiving the action. *Object pronouns* are simply objects put in pronoun form.	*me* *you* *him* *her* *it* *them* *us*	***She*** read to him. ***She*** is the subject pronoun. ***Read*** is the verb. ***Him*** is the object pronoun.

She warned _him_ to buy gas.

Exercise

Exercise 1: Underline the correct _pronoun_ that makes the sentence grammatically correct.

1. _(They_ / _She)_ are going to the store.

2. _(They / She)_ loves to walk in the park.

3. _(You / She)_ have to study for the test tomorrow.

4. _(They / He)_ live in New York City.

5. _(It / They)_ grows very fast.

6. Mike read to _(he /him)._

7. Louis runs with _(she / her)._

8. I need to talk to _(you / she)._

9. The teacher likes to talk to _(us / he)._

10. I returned _(it / us)_ to the library.

Exercise 2: Fill in the blank with the correct _object pronoun._

1. I want to go to a movie tomorrow. You should come with _me_!

2. You have to stay after school. The teacher wants to talk to _____.

3. I forgot my pencil. Lend one to _____.

4. Jeffrey lost his retainer. His mom is going to be really mad at _____.

5. I built a huge snowman. I used mom's old coat to keep _____ warm.

6. She forgot her lunch. I gave half of my sandwich to _____.

7. The cat followed Mary home. She brought _____ inside.

8. You guys are making too much noise! The teacher is going to tell _____ to stop.

9. They want to build a tree house. It would keep _____ busy during the summer.

10. Why is everyone whispering? What secret are you keeping from _____?

Exercise 3: Using both *object and subject pronouns*, fill in the blank using either *I* or *me*.

1. My mom and ⏟ went shopping.

2. Listen to _____.

3. It's time for _____ to go home.

4. _____ have to clean my room before my parents get home.

5. The reward was split between my brother and _____.

6. _____ tried my hardest but I still got a bad grade on my test.

Chapter 12
Personal Pronouns (Part 2)

She *herself* is responsible for purchasing the world's worst copy machine.

12-1 Intensive Pronouns

Definition:	Intensive Pronouns:	Examples:
An *intensive pronoun* puts an emphasis on the other nouns or pronouns in the sentence. Intensive pronouns can be very similar to reflexive pronouns.	*myself* *himself* *herself* *itself* *ourselves* *yourself* *themselves*	1. *He himself* will do the work. (*****Note**: *himself* puts an emphasis on *he* in the sentence.) 2. *She herself* is responsible for the bake sale. 3. *You yourself* are responsible for completing your homework.

12-2 Reflexive Pronouns

Definition:	Reflexive Pronouns:	Examples:
Reflexive pronouns always rename the noun in the sentence. *Note:* intensive pronouns can be very similar to reflexive pronouns.	*myself* *himself* *herself* *itself* *ourselves* *yourself* *themselves*	**1.** Mary looked at ***herself*** in the mirror. (***Note: Mary*** is the *noun* and ***herself*** is the *reflexive pronoun*.) **2.** You must protect ***yourself***. **3.** We must look within ***ourselves*** for courage.

He surprised *himself*! He truly cannot bowl.

Exercise

Exercise 1: Fill in the correct *intensive* or *reflexive noun*.

1. You *yourself* must clean your room.

2. They _____ are responsible for the mess.

3. I _____ am responsible for the car accident.

4. We _____ will have to fix our home.

5. She talks to _____ when she is alone.

6. Mike and I talk to _____ quietly.

7. Have you looked at _____ in the mirror?

8. He must tell _____ he can win the race.

9. I looked at _____ in the reflection* of the car.

10. The dog saw _____ in the mirror and ran away.

*Seeing a picture of something in an object. For example: a mirror.

12-3 Demonstrative Pronouns

Demonstrative pronouns describe the distance you are from specific objects.

Rules:	Demonstrative Pronouns:	Examples:
Use **this** and **these** for objects that you can reach with your hands without getting out of your seat or moving your legs. **This** is singular. **These** is plural. (**Examples: 1 and 2**) Use **that** and **those** for objects that are not close to you. **That** is singular. **Those** is plural. (**Examples: 3 and 4**)	*this* *that* *these* *those*	**1. This** book is in front of me. **2. These** pencils are in front of me. **3. That** restaurant is in another city. **4. Those** cars are down the street.

She hates *those* sticky notes.

Exercise

Exercise 1: Choose the correct *demonstrative pronoun*. Use the word *this, that, these* or *those* to complete the sentence.

1. If you look up the hill, <u>that</u> is my house.

2. _____ keys you are touching are important.

3. _____ restaurants in the other city are expensive.

4. _____ restaurant we are in looks nice.

5. _____ book bag in the other room is mine.

6. _____ award you are touching belongs to my grandfather. Be careful!

7. _____ drinks we are drinking are disgusting.

8. Do not drink _____ drinks on the other side of the room. They are not good.

9. _____ map we are next to is old.

10. _____ trees in Oregon are huge.

12-4 Indefinite Pronouns

Definition:	Indefinite Pronouns:		Examples:
Indefinite pronouns replace nouns that are not specific.	*all*	*another*	**1.** I gave ***all*** my money to him.
	any	*anybody*	**2.** ***Both*** of them are happy.
	anyone	*anything*	**3.** ***Everybody*** must sign the form.
	both	*each*	
	either	*everybody*	
	everyone	*everything*	
	few	*many*	
	neither	*nobody*	
	none	*no one*	
	nothing	*one*	
	several	*some*	
	somebody	*someone*	
	something		

Indefinite Pronoun Rules

All - is 100% of the idea.	***Another*** - is asking you to choose a different option.
Any - is when you don't care which option is chosen.	***Anybody*** - is *anyone*, and there is no preference of what person is chosen. *Any* is the same as *anyone*.
Anyone - is when there is no preference of what person is chosen. *Any* is the same as *anybody*.	***Anything*** - is when there is no preference of what thing is chosen. *Note:* a *thing* is not a person.
Both - includes (two) ideas, things, people, or places.	***Each*** - is when you want to separate, but you still want 100%.

Continued

Either - is when you have two options, and you do not care which option you get.	**Everybody** - is 100% of all the people.
Everyone - is 100% of all the people.	**Everything** - is 100%. *Note:* a *thing* is not a person.
Few - is three (3).	**Many** - is 50% to 70%.
Neither - is when you have two options and you choose nothing.	**Nobody** - is none, and no person will be accepted. Same as *no one*.
None - is 0%.	**No one** - is when no person will be accepted. *No one* is the same as *nobody*.
Nothing - is 0%.	**One** - is simply one (1).
Several - is three (3).	**Some** - is three (3).
Somebody - is when a decision needs to be made on which person is chosen, but you do not care who is chosen.	**Someone** - is an unknown person, and you do not know the person's name.
Something - is when a choice needs to be made on which thing is chosen, but you do not care what is chosen.	

One of them is going to win.

Exercise

everybody	anyone	anything	both	few
something	everyone	no one	nothing	someone

Exercise 1: Using the *indefinite pronouns* in the box below, complete the sentences.

1. Does _anyone_ know what time it is?

2. There is _____ to be afraid of.

3. _____ gets sad once in a while.

4. I would do _____ to get out of washing the dishes!

5. _____ wanted dessert because we all ate too much.

6. Because _____ failed the spelling test, we have to review as a class.

7. _____ Elizabeth and Patricia know how to play the piano.

8. _____ people can name all the state capitals.

9. If you have _____ to say, say it!

10. _____ should teach her a lesson.

Exercise 2: Underline the *indefinite pronoun* for each sentence.

1. Question: Do you want this wine?

   Answer: Yes, give me *(all / everything)* of it.

2. Question: How many people can come?

   Answer: *(Everyone. / All.)*

3. Question: Do you like these two shirts?

   Answer: Yes, I like *(everybody / both)* of them.

4. Question: What items do you want?

   Answer: I want *(nobody / everything)*.

5. Question: How many apple pies do you want?

   Answer: Give me a *(few / everybody)* of them.

6. Question: Is there someone knocking at the door?

   Answer: No, it's *(no one / everyone)*. It's just the wind.

7. Question: Do you want apple or oranges?

   Answer: *(Neither / Everyone)* of them.

8. Comment: The man did not know where the milk was.

   Answer: Ask *(another / everybody)* person.

9. Comment: There are too *(everyone / many)* people at the store.

   Answer: Yea, I know. It's crazy.

10. Comment: *(None / Any)* of my college applications came in the mail today.

    Answer: You must be patient; you just turned them in yesterday.

"*Who* was supposed to fix the water cooler?"

12-5 Interrogative Pronouns

Definition:	Interrogative Pronouns:		Examples:
Interrogative pronouns are used to ask a question.	who what whose whomever whichever	whom which whoever whatever	**Question:** *Who* went to the store? **Answer:** Tom went to the store. **Question:** *Which* of these shirts do you like? **Answer:** I like the one on the left.

Interrogative Pronouns Rules

Who - is used to ask about people.	***Whom*** - can be used to ask about people. It is less usual and more formal than *who*.
What - is used to ask about objects and people.	***Which*** - is used to ask about objects or people.
Whose - is used to ask about the possession of a noun.	***Whoever*** - is used to ask about people, but you are very unsure about the person you are asking about. *Whoever* is only used for people – not objects.
Whomever - is used to ask about people, but used when you want to know who is responsible for a specific action.	***Whatever*** - is used to ask about objects, but you are very unsure about the object you are asking about. *Whatever* is only used for objects – not people.
Whichever - is used to ask about objects or people, but you are very unsure about the person or object you are asking about.	

Whoever continues to give him more work needs to stop.

Exercise

Exercise 1: Choose the correct *interrogative pronoun*.

1. *(Whose / Who)* went to the store?

2. *(Whichever / What)* book did she buy?

3. *(Whom / Whose)* did you ask?

4. *(Whose / Who)* book is this?

5. *(Whoever / Whichever)* stole my book, please give it back.

6. *(Whichever / Whatever)* you want, I will do it.

7. *(Whichever / Whoever)* wants to go to the store, come with me now?

8. *(Whichever / Whomever)* product you want to choose is ok with me.

9. *(Which / Who)* book are you reading?

10. *(What / Who)* is your favorite color?

11. *(Whatever / What)* do you want to eat for dinner?

12. *(Who / Which)* is making all of that noise?

13. *(Who / What)* needs help with homework?

14. *(Which / Who)* of these do you like more?

15. *(Which / Whose)* way do we turn?

16. The bouquet of flowers is for *(whom / which)*?

17. To *(whose / whom)* should I address the envelope?

18. *(Whose / Who)* shoes are in the middle of the floor?

19. *(Whose / Who)* jacket is missing a button?

12-6 Relative Pronouns

Definition:	Relative Pronouns:		Examples:
Relative pronouns connect other noun/pronoun clauses with other parts of a sentence.	who what whose whomever whichever	whom which whoever whatever that	1. The person **who** spilled the coffee must pick it up. 2. The students **that** did not pass the English exam will not pass the class.

Relative Pronouns Rules

Who - is used to ask about people.	***Whom*** - can be used to ask about people. It is less usual and more formal than *who*.
What - is used to ask about objects and people.	***Which*** - is used to ask about objects or people.
Whose - is used to ask about the possession of a noun.	***Whoever*** - is used to ask about people, but you are very unsure about the person you are asking about. *Whoever* is only used for people not objects.
Whomever - is used to ask about people, but used when you want to know who is responsible for a specific action.	***Whatever*** - is used to ask about objects, but you are very unsure about the object you are asking about. *Whatever* is only used for objects not people.
Whichever - is used to ask about objects or people, but you are very unsure about the person or object you are asking about.	***That*** - is used to talk about one specific person, place, thing, or idea.

He does not know *what* is chasing him, but it needs to stop.

Exercise

Exercise 1: Using the *pronoun* definition list provided above choose the correct *relative pronoun*.

1. The person <u>who</u> is driving must remember to fill the car with gas..

2. The person _____ I saw yesterday was tall with dark hair.

3. The direction _____ I want to go is _____ direction you want to go.

4. The person _____ shoes are off must put them on.

5. The man _____ he admires is his father.

Exercise 2: Underline the *relative pronoun* in each sentence.

1. The book <u>that</u> you told me to read is really funny!

2. This is a warning that is difficult to ignore.

3. I'm not sure whose story is the scariest.

4. Because I won first prize in the contest, I can choose whichever prize I want.

5. I rented the apartment that is on Liberty Avenue.

6. I can't believe I ran into the man who found my missing purse.

7. Is there a place where I can buy a new hat?

8. I don't know what happened.

9. This is the man whose wife was my teacher.

10. Bring me the book that is on the table.

Chapter 13
The Possessives

She has toilet paper stuck to *herself*, but she is still having a wonderful day.

13-1 The Possessives

Possessives show ownership of a specific subject, and can be written in pronoun or adjective form.

Rules:	Examples:		Sample Sentences:
Possessive pronouns are words that stand by themselves. There is no noun behind them.	**Singular**	**Plural**	**1.** The pencil is ***mine***.
	mine	*ours*	**2.** That test is ***hers***.
	yours	*yours*	
	hers/his	*theirs*	
	its		
Possessive adjectives do not stand by themselves. Possessive adjectives are placed directly in front of the noun.	***my*** book ***your*** book ***his/her/its*** book	***our*** books ***your*** books ***their*** books	**1.** ***My*** hair is brown. **2.** ***Your*** pen is on the table.

Continued

> *Note:* All possessive nouns will have apostrophes after them. All possessives pronouns will not have apostrophes after them.
>
> **Examples:**
> *possessive noun:* That football is the **school's**.
> *possessive adjective:* That football is **mine**.

Exercise

Exercise 1: Underline the correct *possessive pronoun* for each sentence. Look at the noun(s) in bold to help you choose your answer.

1. That book belongs to **me**, so that book is *(mine / theirs)*.

2. That pencil belongs to **him**, so that book is *(hers / his)*.

3. Those shoes belong to **us**, so those shoes are *(his / ours)*.

4. These keys belong to **them**, so these keys are *(theirs / his)*.

5. The radio belongs to **her**, so the radio is *(hers / theirs)*.

6. This book bag belongs to **Mike**, so this book bag is *(his / hers)*.

7. The notepads belong to the **church**; these notepads are *(theirs / his)*.

8. The cell phone belongs to **Susan**, so the cell phone is *(hers / theirs)*.

9. The statue belongs to the **city**, so the statue is *(hers / theirs)*.

10. The books belong to **him and me**, so the book is *(ours / his)*.

Exercise 2: Underline the *possessive pronoun* in the sentence.

1. The paper is yours.

2. Those books are theirs, but you can borrow them.

3. That watch is hers.

4. These clothes are ours, but we're giving them away.

5. The iPod is mine.

Exercise 3: Underline the *possessive adjectives* in the sentence.

1. <u>Your</u> book is on the table.

2. My pencil is dull.* *(*dull: not sharp)*

3. Your TV is on.

4. If you eat that candy, your teeth will rot. (rot = be bad)

5. My iPod is broken.

Chapter 14
Questions

Question: "*Don't* you like fixing floors?"
Answer: "*No*, he hates it."

14-1 Negative Questions

Definition:	Example Questions:	Example Answers:
Negative questions are used when you ask a question and you want "yes" as an answer. Sometimes the answer may be "no," but you are still looking for "yes." There are two ways to write negative questions.	**Question: *Don't* you know** how to read? **Question: *Do you not* know** how to read? **Question: *Doesn'*t he want to** travel? **Question: *Does he not* want** to travel?	**Answer: *Yes*, I know how to** read. **Answer: *No*, he doesn't want** to travel.

Exercise

Exercise 1: Re-write the following questions to make two *negative questions*.

    1. Did you study for the test?

        Did you not study for the test?

        Didn't you study for the test?

2. Can you ask her for help?

   _____

   _____

3. Will you join us for dinner?

   _____

   _____

4. Do you want more time?

   _____

   _____

5. Could you wait ten more minutes?

   _____

   _____

6. Are they serving pizza today in the cafeteria?

   _____

   _____

7. Do you like roller coasters?

   _____

   _____

Exercise 2: Answer the following *negative questions* using a complete sentence.

1. Won't you miss seeing me every day? *(No)*

   No, I will not miss seeing you every day.

2. Aren't you tired? *(Yes)*

   _____

3. Doesn't he have two cats? *(Yes)*

_____

4. Is she not from Canada? *(Yes)*

_____

5. Aren't you the oldest of five children? *(No)*

_____

6. Have you not eaten cereal every day for the past year? *(No)*

_____

14-2 Yes / No Questions

Definition:	Examples:
A *yes* or *no* question is a question that can be answered with a *yes* or a *no*.	**Question:** Do like chocolate ice cream? **Answer:** *Yes*, I like chocolate. *No*, I like vanilla. *No*, I do not like chocolate ice cream.

Exercise

Exercise 1: Answer *yes* or *no* to all the personal questions about yourself.

1. Question: Are you learning English?

   Answer: Yes, I am learning English.

2. Question: Do you like to read?

   Answer: _____

3. Question: Is your eye color brown?

   Answer: _____

4. Question: Do you have a sister?

   Answer: _____

5. Question: Do you have a cell phone?

   Answer: _____

14-3 Question Words

Question words are used to get information. They include *who, what, when, where, why, how, which* and *whose*.

Question Word:	Rules:	Examples:
Who	*Who* is asking about a specific person and is used as the subject of the sentence. A *singular verb* almost always follows *who* in the sentence.	*Who* took my pencil?
What	*What* can be used as the subject of the sentence. (**Example 1**) *What* can be used as the object of the sentence. (**Example 2**) *What* can come before a noun in a sentence. (**Example 3**) *What kind of* is used when a speaker needs to make a decision about the type of object they want. (**Example 4**) *What + do* is used to ask for information about the subject. (**Example 5**) *What + verb* can be used to ask information about an action that is being performed. (**Example 6**)	1. *What's* wrong? 2. She said *what*? 3. *What* time is it? 4. **What** *kind* **of** cereal do you want? 5. *What* does she want? 6. *What* is she doing upstairs?
When	A speaker uses *when* to ask a question about time?	*When* do you want to leave?

Continued

Question Word:	Rules:	Examples:
Where	A speaker uses *where* to ask questions about a place or about the place of noun.	1. *Where* do you want to go? 2. *Where's* Oregon?
Why	A speaker uses *why* to ask for explanation about a subject.	**Why** are there 50 stars on the American Flag?
How	A speaker uses *how* to describe directions. (**Example 1**) A speaker also uses *how* to understand the amount of time it takes to do an action. (**Example 2**) A speaker uses *how often* to understand the amount of times an action is being performed. (**Example 3**) A speaker uses *how far* to describe the distance of a subject. (**Example 4**) A speaker uses *how much* to ask the quantity of a certain subject. (**Example 5**)	1. *How* do you speak English? 2. *How* long does it take to learn English? 3. *How* often do you go to restaurants? 4. *How* far is Washington, DC to California? 5. *How much* money do you have?
Which	A speaker uses *which*, when he/she is making a choice from a specific number of possibilities.	There are 19 cars. *Which* car do you want?
Whose	A speaker uses *whose*, when wanting to know the person that owns a <u>noun</u>.	*Whose* book is this?

How much money does he have?

Sentence Structure Formulas:

Who + *is* + *gerund* + *preposition*
Who *is talking to* Jackie?

What + *noun* + *auxiliary verb*
What *time is* it?

When + *auxiliary verb* + *pronoun* + *main verb?*
When *are you leaving?*

Where + *auxiliary verb* + *my* + *noun?*
Where *is my book?*

Why + *auxiliary verb* + *pronoun* + *adjective?*
Why *are you happy?*

How + *adjective* + *auxiliary verb* + *pronoun?*
How *old are you?*

Whose + *noun* + *auxiliary verb* + *this/these?*
Whose *notebook is this?*

Why **does he own so many clothes?**

Exercise

Exercise 1: Write the correct *question word* for each question.

1. Question: <u>Who</u> is the woman?

   Answer: She is my mother.

2. Question: _____ time is it?

   Answer: It's three o'clock.

3. Question: _____ are you leaving?

   Answer: I am leaving at 7 A.M.

4. Question: _____ is my book?

   Answer: It's on the table.

5. Question: _____ are you happy?

   Answer: I did well in school.

6. Question: _____ do you draw?

   Answer: With lots of practice.

7. Question: _____ notebook is this?

   Answer: It's Tom's notebook.

Exercise 2: You have been given a once-in-a-lifetime chance to travel back in time and interview Ben Franklin. Read the paragraph below, and answer the questions.

I am so excited! I just created a time machine, and it is going to let me go back in time and interview Ben Franklin. I'll be traveling back to July, 1776, and will talk to him just after the Declaration of Independence would have been signed. I will be in Philadelphia. Even though Franklin has done a lot in his life, I want to talk to him about the drafting and signing of the Declaration of Independence. I'm a little worried that he will be scared of me if tell him I'm from the future, but once I explain everything to him, I actually think he'll be really excited. I will just sit him down and tell him the truth. He was an inventor, so I'm sure he will be fascinated by my time machine. He will probably have a lot of questions for me. I wonder if he will want to come back to the future with me. I would for sure get an "A" on my history project if I brought him in to class to talk.

My paper is due on January 17. I chose Ben Franklin because his birthday is actually also on January 17. Plus, he's really interesting.

1. Whom are you going to interview?

   I am going to interview Ben Franklin.

2. Where will the interview take place?

   _____

3. Why do you want to interview this person?

   _____

4. What date will you need to set the time machine to?

   _____

5. How do you plan to explain to Ben Franklin that you come from the future?

   _____

6. When will your paper be ready?

   _____

7. Why did you choose Ben Franklin as the subject of your paper?

   _____

8. What grade do you hope to get on your paper?

_____

9. What will you try to do to get an "A" on your paper?

_____

10. What important document did Franklin help draft and sign?

_____

Exercise 3: Work in pairs. You are a journalist. Interview your classmate to see what person they would like to meet the most. (The person does not need to be currently living. It can be anyone in history.) Write down your classmate's response.

1. Whom are you going to meet?

_____

2. Where would you like to meet this person?

_____

3. Why do you want to meet this person?

_____

4. What are you and the person going do when you meet.

_____

5. When would you like to meet this person?

_____

Chapter 15
Prepositions and Prepositional Phrases

She needs *to* relax.

15-1 Prepositions of Time

Prepositions:	Sentence Structure Formulas:	Examples:
at	*at* + a specific time	**1.** The movie starts *at* 8:00pm.
	at + night	**2.** My class is *at* 8:15am.
in	*in* + month	**1.** Seth was born *in* May.
	in + year	**2.** She was born *in* 1980.
	in + the morning	**3.** You have soccer practice *in* the morning.
	in + the afternoon	**4.** Your dentist appointment is *in* the afternoon.
	in + the evening	**5.** They have a party *in* the evening
on	*on* + day of the week	**1.** I go back to school *on* Monday.
	on + date of the month	**2.** I was born *on* July 3, 1984.

Continued

Prepositions:	Sentence Structure Formulas:	Examples:
from/to	*From* (a specific time) *to* a (specific time)	I go to school *from* 8:00am *to* 3:00pm every day.
after	*after* + noun	I will not leave work until *after* 5:00pm.

15-2 Prepositions of Place

Prepositions:	Sentence Structure Formulas:	Examples:
at	*at* + the place	They are *at* the grocery store. **Note: at* is most commonly used when you are standing next to something, but not actually in it.
in	*in* + the (object)	The family is *in* the car.
on	*on* + the (object)	The children are singing *on* the stage.
next to	*next to* + the (object)	The children are *next to* the school.
under	*under* + the (object)	The gondola is going *under* the bridge. **Note: gondola = boat*
between	*between* + (object) <u>and</u> (object).	The woman in white is *between* the woman in the green <u>and</u> the woman in the red.
on top of	*on top of* + the (object)	The car is *on top of* the world.
opposite	*opposite* + adjective + preposition + (object) *opposite* + preposition + (object)	1. The women are sitting *on* opposite sides of the table. 2. The women are *opposite of* each other.
behind	*behind* + the (object)	The girl is *behind* the desk.
through	*through* + the (object).	The train is going *through* the tunnel.
over	*over* + the (object).	Take the bridge to go *over* the river.

15-3 Prepositions of Movement

Prepositions:	Sentence Structure Formulas:	Examples:
to	*to* + the (object) *to* + verb	1. He's carrying the garbage *to* the trash can. 2. I wanted *to* drive.
through	*through* + the (object)	The man looked *through* the telescope.
across	*across* + the (object)	The pretty woman is walking *across* the street.
along	*along* + the (object)	The couple is walking *along* the trail.
down	*down* + the (object)	The woman walked *down* the aisle.
over	*over* + the (object)	The Italian flag is hung *over* the bridge.
off	*off* *(sentence ending)* *off* + the object.	1. In the morning, I turn my alarm clock *off*. 2. Get *off* the stage.
around	*around* + the (object)	The pilot will fly the plane *around* the world.
into	*into* + the (object)	The wine is being poured *into* the glass.

He is nervous *about* buying stocks.

Prepositions List

A.	**C.**	**M.**	**T.**
aboard	concerning	minus	than
about	considering		through
above		**N.**	to
across	**D.**	near	toward
after	despite		towards
against	down	**O.**	
along	during	of	**U.**
amid		off	under
among	**E.**	on	underneath
anti	except	onto	unlike
around	excepting	opposite	until
as	excluding	outside	up
at		over	upon
	F.		
B.	following	**P.**	**V.**
before	for	past	versus
behind	from	per	via
below		plus	
beneath	**I.**		**W.**
beside	in	**R.**	with
besides	inside	round	within
between	into	regarding	without
beyond			
but	**L.**	**S.**	
by	like	since	

Exercise

Exercise 1: Write the correct *preposition*.

1. I walked <u>to</u> the store.

2. The movie starts _____ 8:10pm.

3. The restaurant is open _____ the evenings only.

4. His birthday is _____ Saturday.

5. We usually have dinner _____ 8:00pm.

6. He leaves for New York _____ Friday.

7. My plane leaves _____ midnight.

8. They return _____ April 24.

9. We usually go _____ vacation _____ the summer.

10. He went to California _____ July.

Exercise 2: Write the correct *preposition*.

1. I am leaving *in* six days.

2. I go to work early _____ the morning.

3. They eat breakfast _____ the morning.

4. The metro leaves promptly _____ time.

5. Will we be too late _____ catch the train?

6. You were not _____ time for work this morning.

7. I have _____ work _____ 8:00am _____ 5:00pm every day.

8. Don't be late! Be _____ time for the start of the class.

9. What were you doing _____ the 1980's?

10. We always stay up late _____ New Year's Eve.

Exercise 3: Write the correct *preposition*.

1. Go *down* the street and pick up some milk.

2. She walked _____ the store to buy some groceries.

3. You must walk _____ the bridge to get to the store.

4. You can walk _____ the lake.

5. The salesperson said the product was _____ the aisle.

6. You must turn the lights _____ in order to save money.

7. The coffee shop is _____ the corner.

8. Put the money _____ your pocket.

9. Turn the lights _____ so I can see.

10. You must look _____ the binoculars in order to see closer.

15-4 Adjective + Preposition Followed by a Gerund

Rule:	Sentence Structure Formula:	Examples:
Using the rules of the prepositions taught earlier, use *adjective + preposition followed by a gerund* in order to express the way you feel about a certain action.	*adjective + preposition + gerund*	1. Nick is ***tired of running***. 2. Ashley is ***nervous about testing***.

Exercise

Column A					
afraid	bored	disappointed	guilty	happy	interested
known	worried	proud	remembered	responsible	scared

Column B					
about	for	in	of	to	with

Exercise 1: Choose an *adjective* from column A or a *preposition* from column B to complete the sentences below.

1. I am <u>afraid</u> *of making* a mistake.

2. Kelly is *happy* _____ *winning* first place.

3. Tina is _____ *for collecting* money for our class trip.

4. Everyone is _____ *about failing* the test.

5. I am *guilty* _____ *eating* too much at Thanksgiving.

6. We are all _____ *in placing* last.

7. I am _____ *of getting* lost in a new town.

8. Tony is *bored* _____ *listening* to his sister play piano.

9. We are all *responsible* _____ *making* our own lunches.

10. Kelly will be _____ *for singing* off-key in the musical. It was awful!

15-5 Verb + Preposition Followed by a Gerund

Rule:	Sentence Structure Formula:	Examples:
Use a *verb + preposition followed by a gerund* to give the preposition an action.	*verb + preposition + gerund*	1. We ***talked about hiking***. 2. ***I'm interested in being*** an astronaut.

Exercise

concentrate on	rely on	warned against	begin by
dreamt about	thanks for	pay for	agree with
escape from	use for	apologize for	worry about

Exercise 1: Using the word box above, complete the sentences with the correct <u>verb</u> and <u>preposition</u> combination.

Dear Uncle David and Aunt Lucy,

Let me <u>begin by</u> telling you how great it was to see you at my birthday party. It was great to see you both, and Uncle David, you looked great in your new suit and tie. That being said, let me _____ spilling my red punch all over your clothes. I also am sorry that you were hit with so many paintball pellets. I think we were all just trying to _____ shooting anyone who came past us, and when you walked through the playing field, we assumed it was to be part of the fun, not because you were trying to get to your car to change your clothes. You should have been _____ getting so dressed up for an eleven-year-old's party, especially when its theme is "paintball."

_____ giving me a check for my birthday. For the last year, I have _____ buying a television for my bedroom, and initially, any money I had I would

_____ making that happen. It would be an _____ living in a house full of eight older sisters and not having to _____ fighting over the remote every time I want to watch my favorite TV show. (I never get to choose what to watch.)

After hearing about how much money your suit cost, my mom is insisting that I pay for you to buy a new suit. Even though I don't _____ making a kid _____ buying a grown-up a new suit (again, the theme was paintball), I will. That being said, I will _____ seeing photos of the new suit to know this is what the money was used for.

Sincerely,
Joseph

15-6 Noun + Preposition Followed by a Gerund

Rule:	Sentence Structure Formula:	Examples:
Use *noun + preposition followed by a gerund* to give more information about the subject.	*noun + preposition + gerund*	1. The ***author's book about running*** was very good. 2. We had a ***conversation about fishing***.

Exercise

Exercise 1: Make the underlined phrase into a *gerund*.

1. process of <u>to sew</u>

   <u>process of sewing</u>

2. story about <u>to build</u>

   _____

3. love of <u>to read</u>

   _____

4. fear of <u>to fly</u>

   _____

5. delay in <u>to play</u>

_____

6. reputation for <u>to sing</u>

_____

7. memory of <u>to swim</u>

_____

Exercise 2: Use the phrases above to complete the sentences.

1. I can't figure out the <u>process of sewing</u>, so my shirt is missing three buttons.

2. My mom has a _____. We drive everywhere for vacation.

3. She has a _____ movies in 3D.

4. I just read a _____ skyscrapers.

5. She has a _____ incredibly off-key.

6. The rain has caused a _____ the championship game.

15-7 Subordinate Clauses

Definition:	Examples:

Subordinate clauses are dependent clauses that start with subordinate conjunctions or relative pronouns.	**_After I go to the store_**, _I will go to the library_.
	    subordinate clause independent clause
	
	Whoever spilled the milk, _please clean it up_.
	    subordinate clause independent clause
	
	Since I got a tutor, _my grades have improved_.
	    subordinate clause independent clause

Once he builds this pool, _he's asking for his money back._

List of Subordinate Conjunctions

after	*although*	*as*	*because*
before	*even if*	*even though*	*if*
in order that	*once*	*provided that*	*rather than*
since	*so that*	*than*	*that*
though	*unless*	*until*	*when*
whenever	*where*	*whereas*	*wherever*
whether	*while*	*why*	

Exercise

even though	although	because	until after	if

Exercise 1: Use the *subordinate clauses* below to complete the sentences. *Note: Some sentences will use more than one.*

1. Don't brush your teeth *until after* you've finished your orange juice.

2. _____ the cake looked delicious, it tasted terrible.

3. I have to make sure my sister doesn't miss the bus _____ if she is late one more time, she will get a detention.

4. _____ you are going to the store, will you please buy milk?

5. I will wait for you after school _____ I don't want to miss my favorite TV show.

Exercise 2: Underline the *subordinate clauses* in each sentence.

1. <u>After</u> the play ended, the audience applauded.

2. I don't want to go to the party unless Shelly is invited as well.

3. You are eating peas tonight whether you want to or not.

4. Even though I set three alarms this morning, I still managed to be late for my interview.

5. Once you start eating potato chips, it's hard to stop.

"<u>After I quit my job</u>, I'm going on a vacation."

15-8 Verb + Preposition

Rule:	Sentence Structure Formula:	Examples:
Use *verb + preposition* to give the preposition an action.	*verb + preposition*	**1.** She's ***putting on*** her new shoes. **2.** Michael's ***running around*** me.

Exercise

Exercise 1: Underline the *verb + preposition* in each sentence below.

1. I am <u>asking for</u> help.

2. We have agreed on a price for the baseball card.

3. Jessica will apologize for yelling at you.

4. We can't argue about everything!

5. My mom decided to care for my grandfather after he had a stroke.

6. I belong to three different teams.

7. I don't care about the weather! We play inside!

8. Do you still communicate with your old neighbor?

9. I will apply for an after-school job.

10. I still believe in the tooth fairy.

Chapter 16
Noun Usage

She works hard on the *computer*.

16-1 Proper and Common Nouns

Definition:	Examples:
A *proper noun* names a specific person, place, thing or idea. A proper noun is always capitalized.	**Person:** *Tom* **Place:** *United States of America* **Thing:** *Statue of Liberty* **Idea:** *Albert Einstein's Theory of Relativity*
Common nouns are nouns naming a general person, place, thing, or idea. Common nouns are not capitalized.	**Person:** *student* **Place:** *school* **Thing:** *desk* **Idea:** *thinking about going to a party.*

Exercise

Exercise 1: Is each noun a *common* or *proper noun*? Underline the correct answer.

1. Eiffel Tower *(common / proper)*

2. The White House *(common / proper)*

3. clock *(common / proper)*

4. New York Times *(common / proper)*

5. Mike *(common / proper)*

6. English *(common / proper)*

7. Los Angeles, CA *(common / proper)*

8. bank *(common / proper)*

9. United States *(common / proper)*

10. Tuesday *(common / proper)*

16-2 Irregular Nouns

Definition:	Examples:
Many nouns have irregular plural forms. Irregular nouns are nouns that completely change the spelling of the word when the word is in plural form.	one *child* = two *children* one *man* = three *men* one *person* = four *people* one *woman* = five *women*

Examples of Irregular Nouns

The ending of the noun changes from -*us* to –*i*

Singular:	*alumnus*	*cactus*	*fungus*	*nucleus*
Plural:	*alumni*	*cacti*	*fungi*	*nuclei*

The ending of the noun changes from -*is* to -*es*

Singular:	*axis*	*analysis*	*basis*	*crisis*
Plural:	*axes*	*analyses*	*bases*	*crises*

The ending of the noun changes from -*ix* to -*ices* or -*ex* to -*eces*

Singular:	*appendix*	*index*	*matrix*
Plural:	*appendices*	*indexes*	*matrixes*

The ending of the noun changes from -*eu* to -*eaux*

Singular:	*bureau*
Plural:	*bureaus*

The ending of noun changes to -*en*

Singular:	*child*	*man*	*ox*	*woman*
Plural:	*children*	*men*	*oxen*	*women*

* *Note:* Some words have more than one plural form. *Fungi = funguses, indexes = indeces, matrixes = matrices, and bureaus = bureaux.*

The ending of the noun changes to *-a*			
Singular:	*bacterium*	*curriculum*	*medium*	*memorandum*
Plural:	*bacteria*	*curricula*	*media*	*memoranda*

Nouns that have no change			
Singular:	*deer*	*fish*	*sheep*	*series*
Plural:	*deer*	*fish*	*sheep*	*series*

The middle of the noun changes from *-oo* to *-ee*		
Singular:	*foot*	*goose*	*tooth*
Plural:	*feet*	*geese*	*teeth*

The ending of the noun changes from *-a* to *-ae*			
Singular:	*antenna*	*formula*	*nebula*	*vertebra*
Plural:	*antennae**	*formulas**	*nebulae*	*vertebrae*

The ending of the noun changes from *-ouse* to *-ice*	
Singular:	*mouse*	*louse*
Plural:	*mice*	*lice*

* Note: *Antennae = antennas, and formulas = formulae.*

Her *feet* are in a lot of pain.

Exercise

Exercise 1: You must change the *regular noun* to an *irregular noun*.

    1. foot = *feet*

    2. man = _____

    3. child = _____

    4. woman = _____

    5. mouse = _____

    6. fish = _____

    7. sheep = _____

    8. tooth = _____

    9. curriculum = _____

    10. deer = _____

    11. louse = _____

16-3 Compound Nouns

Compound nouns are two words combined together to make one word or phrase.

There are Three Forms of Compound Nouns:

Definitions:	Examples:	
Closed Form - Words are put together to make one word and there is no hyphen between the words.	*firefly*	*keyboard*
	secondhand	*makeup*
	softball	*notebook*
	motorcycle	*childlike*
Hyphenated Form - A word phrase that has one definition, with a hyphen between each word.	*daughter-in-law*	*six-pack*
	master-at-arms	*six-year-old*
	over-the-counter	*mass-produced*
Open Form - A word phrase that has one definition. There is no hyphen between the words.	*post office*	*real estate*
	upper class	*full moon*
	half sister	*attorney general*

The *golf ball* is right where he wants it.

Exercise

boat	dream	back	time	fight
hopper	ball	pike	spoon	mother

Exercise 1: Complete the *compound noun* using the word box above.

    1. foot *ball*

    2. day _____

    3. grass _____

    4. grand _____

    5. day _____

    6. dog _____

    7. quarter _____

    8. sail _____

    9. tea _____

    10. turn _____

Chapter 17
Advanced Nouns

We went to the amusement park for _Mom's_ birthday.

17-1 Forming Possessives

Definitions:	Sentence Structure Formula:	Examples:
The _possessive_ gives ownership to nouns. The possessive shows who owns the noun.	_noun_ + _'s_ _Mike_ + _'s_ = _Mike's_	**Question:** Is this _your_ pencil? **Answer:** No, it's _David's_ pencil. **Question:** Is this _Mike's_ car? **Answer:** Yes, it's _Mike's_ car. **Question:** What holiday is it? **Answer:** _Mother's_ Day.
Possessive proper nouns that end in _-s_ will end with _-s'_. *A proper noun is the name of a person or object. (**Example:** _Statue of Liberty / Ashley_)	_noun_ + _s'_ _Mike_ + _'s_ = _Mike's_	1. _Tess'_ car 2. _Charles'_ pencil
Last names also use _-'s_ when forming the possessive.	_last name_ + _'s_	1. It's _Mr. Smith's_ hat. 2. He's _Mr. Young's_ son.

Exercise

Exercise 1: Complete the sentences with the correct form of the *possessive*.

1. **(Seth)**   Mike had gone to <u>Seth's</u> house because

2. **(Mike)**   _____ car had broken down and he needed to call a tow truck.

3. **(Seth)**   _____ phone wasn't working so Seth had gone to Mike's next-door-neighbor – Louis.

4. **(Louis)**   _____ phone was working and Mike called a tow truck.

   While Mike was waiting for the tow truck, there were many boys outside playing.

5. **(boy)**   The _____ ball had been stuck in a tree.

6. **(Ben)**   A boy walked over to Mike and said "_____ ball was in a tree,

7. **(Mike)**   and with _____ help, the boys could get the ball out of the tree."

8. **(tree)**   Mike went to the tree and climbed up the _____ thick branches.

   Mike got the ball and after he climbed down the tree, the boy said, "thank you."

9. **(Mike)**   At that moment, _____ tow truck came and Mike left with the repairperson.

Tom's **first vacation was a good one.**

17-2 Count and Noncount Nouns

Definitions:	Examples:	Examples:	Example Sentences:
Count nouns are any nouns that you can count one by one. You add an *-s* at the end of the word to make a count noun, plural. A count noun may have *a* or *an* in front of it.	**Singular** *a chair* *a cup* *a book*	**Plural** *a few chairs* *five cups* *three books*	1. I bought a <u>few</u> **chairs**. 2. He asked for <u>five</u> **cups** of soda. 3. I read <u>three</u> **books** at the library.
Noncount nouns are nouns that you <u>cannot</u> count one by one. You <u>do not</u> add an *-s* at the end of the word to make a count noun, plural. A count noun may <u>not</u> have *a* or *an* in front of it. With noncount nouns use *a little, some, too much,* or *a lot of*.	**Singular** *water* *milk* *sugar*	**Plural** *water* *milk* *sugar*	**Correct:** Can I have <u>some</u> ***water?*** **Incorrect:** Can I have ~~a few~~ ***water?*** **Correct:** I want <u>a little</u> ***milk***. **Incorrect:** I want ~~three~~ ***milk***. **Correct:** Don't use <u>too much</u> ***sugar***. **Incorrect:** Don't use ~~four~~ ***sugar***.

Exercise

Exercise 1: Look at the *noun* below. If it is a *count noun*, write *count* on the line. If it is a *noncount noun*, write *noncount*.

1. glass <u>noncount</u>

2. flour _____

3. flower _____

4. chalkboard _____

5. chalk _____

6. soccer _____

7. soccer ball _____

8. poetry _____

9. homework _____

10. assignment _____

Exercise 2: Is the highlighted word a *noncount* or a *count noun*?

1. Can I have some *coffee*? *noncount noun*

2. I love your *furniture*. _____

3. Do you have a *pencil*? _____

4. I don't have any *money*. _____

5. Drink lots of *water*. _____

6. I love listening to *CD's*. _____

7. There is too much *oil* on my pizza. _____

8. Eat an *apple* instead of a *cookie*. _____

9. Do you have a *pair of scissors*? _____

10. They dug a huge *hole*. _____

Chapter 18
Noun Clauses

"I am happy that you are *quick to act*, but I am happier that I am quicker."
Note: quick to act = fast to move

18-1 Noun Clauses

Definition:	Examples:
A *clause* is a group of words that have a subject and verb within the same group. Simply, a *noun clause* can take the place of the noun in a sentence.	**1.** He *is glad to be* done. **2.** They *were good to go*. **3.** She was *quick to act*.

There are Three Different Kinds of Noun Clauses:

1. A noun clause that starts with *whether* or *if*

2. A noun clause that starts with a *question*

3. A noun clause that starts with the word *that*

18-2 A Noun Clause that Starts with *whether* or *if*

Rule:	Examples:
Noun clauses that start with **whether** or **if** are used to answer questions that you do not know the answer to. **Whether** and **if** are usually interchangeable.	**Question:** Is her dad a teacher? **Answer:** I don't know **if** her dad is a teacher. **Question:** Are you going to the party? **Answer:** I don't know **whether** I'm going to the party. **Question:** Is he okay? **Answer:** I don't know **if** he's hurt or not.

"I don't know *whether* I should allow you to board the plane with this mysterious box."

Exercise

Exercise 1: Finish the sentence. Start each noun clause with *whether* or *if*.

1. Question: Does she live in Ohio?

   Answer: I don't know: <u>whether she lives in Ohio</u>.

2. Question: Are you going to the movies later?

   Answer: I don't know: _____.

3. Question: Is she a Native American?

   Answer: I don't know: _____.

4. Question: Can they go to the restaurant later?

   Answer: I don't know: _____.

5. Question: Does Mike have an extra pencil?

   Answer: I don't know: _____.

6. Question: Are Mike and Sam still fighting?

   Answer: I don't know: _____.

7. Question: Does anyone know whether it will rain today?

   Answer: I don't know: _____.

8. Question: Is Thomas still in the hospital?

   Answer: I don't know: _____.

9. Question: Are you all still going to California?

   Answer: I don't know: _____.

10. Question: Is she hurt?

    Answer: I don't know: _____.

18-3 A Noun Clause that Starts with a Question Word

Rule:	Examples:
Noun clauses that start with a *question word* are usually used to answer a question about the subject.	**Question:** *Where* does she live? **Answer:** I don't know *where* she lives. **Question:** *How* do you speak French? **Answer:** I don't know *how* to speak French. **Question:** *Who* is the man in the green shirt? **Answer:** I don't know *who* the man is. **Question:** *When* are you going back to school? **Answer:** I don't know *when* I'm going back to school. **Question:** *Why* is she writing a book? **Answer:** I don't know *why* she's writing a book.

*"**How** did I get this job?"*

Exercise

Exercise 1: Complete the sentence with the correct *noun clause*.

1. Question: *Where* does Tom live?

   Answer: I don't know: <u>where Tom lives</u>.

2. Question: *Who* is going to be at your party?

   Answer: I don't know: _____.

3. Question: *How* do you make bread?

   Answer: I don't know: _____.

4. Question: *When* are you going to the supermarket?

   Answer: I don't know: _____.

5. Question: *Why* is she cleaning?

   Answer: I don't know: _____.

6. Question: *Where* is Oregon?

   Answer: I know: _____.

7. Question: *Who* is at the door?

   Answer: I know who's: _____.

8. Question: *How* do you ride a bike?

   Answer: I don't know: _____.

9. Question: *When* are they going to New York City?

   Answer: I know: _____.

10. Question: *Why* is she laughing?

    Answer: I know: _____.

18-4 A Noun Clause that Starts with the Word *That*

Rule:	Examples:
Noun clauses that start with the word *that* are used to answer questions in which a person who is answering is thinking or giving an opinion. *Note: That* will usually come directly before the pronoun or common noun in the sentence.	**1.** I think *that* she's nice. (**Note: she's* a pronoun.) **2.** I know *that* answer. (**Note: answer* is a common noun. **3.** I think *that* you are smart. . (**Note: you* is a pronoun.)

I think *that* she used too much white-out.

Exercise

Exercise 1: Rewrite each sentence placing the word *that* in the sentence.

1. Question: Is Oregon hot this time of year?

   Answer: I think it definitely is.

   Answer: <u>I think that it definitely is.</u>

2. Question: Is Dr. Walker a good physician?

   Answer: I think he's a great physician.

   Answer: _____

3. Question: I this juice good?

   Answer: I think it's pretty good.

   Answer: _____

4. Question: Are the trees in the United States large?

   Answer: I know they're very large.

   Answer: _____

5. Statement: I think that the U.S. is a small country.

   Answer: I think it's a huge country.

   Answer: _____

6. Statement: I love the French language.

   Answer: I think it's a beautiful language.

   Answer: _____

7. Statement: I believe in God.

   Answer: I think he's real.

   Answer: _____

8. Statement: I never understand him.

   Answer: I think he's difficult to understand also.

   Answer: _____

9. Statement: Is New York a nice city to visit?

   Answer: I think it's a wonderful city to visit.

   Answer: _____

10. Statement: I believe in ghosts.

    Answer: I don't. I think that they're fake.

    Answer: _____

Chapter 19
Modals (Part 1)

"I'm about to leave. I *should* not answer it."

19-1 Modal Auxiliaries and Similar Expressions

Definition:	Examples:		
Modals are words used to explain a speaker's emotions or attitude towards an object or idea.			*can* go
			could go
The *modal auxiliaries* in the American English language are ***can, could, had better, has/have to, may, might, must, ought to, shall, should, will,*** and ***would.***	*I*		*had better* go
	We		*has/have to* go
	You		*may* go
	They	+	*might* go
	He		*must* go
	She		*ought* to go
	It		*shall* go
	I		*should* go
			will go
			would go

Continued

Rules:	Examples:
Modals will never be put in the plural form.	**Correct:** I *might* go to the store. **Incorrect:** I *mights* go to the store.
Modals always come before the simple form of a verb.	**Correct:** I must*(modal)* go*(verb)*. **Incorrect:** I go*(verb)* must*(modal)*.

More on Must, Have to and Have got to

Rules:	Examples:
Must, *have got to* and *have* to express a need to do a certain action *Must* is considered to be more formal. *Have to* is considered to be more informal and is more commonly used in everyday American speech.	1. I *have to* study tonight. 2. All employees *must* wash their hands. 3. I *have to* clean my room. 4. You *must* clean your room before you go. 5. *You have got to* pay that bill today.

Rules of Modals:

can: be able to
could: be able to *(past tense of can)* or to suggest an idea
had better: be sure to perform
has/have to: no or little choice
may: polite request or stating an action will possibly happen in the future
might: something is true and could happen in the future
must: rule or law, you have no choice
ought to: good idea that you should perform the action
shall: it will happen in the future
should: good idea that the action happens in the future

*"**Shall** we stay in the pool, or *should* we get out."*

Exercise

would	must	could	ought to	shall
will	have to	may	can	would

Exercise 1: Using the choices in the box, fill in the blank with the correct *modal auxiliary*.

1. <u>Would</u> you go to the store and buy a pound of sugar?

2. I _____ name all fifty states alphabetically.

3. _____ I please borrow a pencil?

4. You _____ wear a jacket. It's freezing!

5. Jessica was full. She _____ not eat another bite.

6. Do I _____ sit with Aunt Judy? She always teases me.

7. You _____ put more air in your front tire.

8. _____ you please turn the music down?

9. _____ I call the nurse?

10. _____ you please stop tapping your pencil on the desk?

Exercise 2: Rewrite each sentence using the statement provided and the *modal auxiliary* in parentheses.

1. You are asking politely to use the restroom. *(may)*

   May I go to the restroom?

2. You are suggesting to your friend that it's a good idea to read a book. *(ought to)*

   _____

3. You played the piano when you were five. *(used to)*

   _____

4. You need to clean your room before your parents get home. *(will)*

   _____

5. You are looking for your retainer. *(need)*

   _____

6. You are asking your friend to dance with you. *(shall)*

   _____

7. You are suggesting to your friend to take the bus to her house. *(could)*

   _____

8. Tell your friend you are able to juggle. *(can)*

   _____

9. Tell your friend that he/she has no choice except to brush his/her teeth every day. *(must)*

   _____

10. Tell your friends that they have no choice but to study. *(have to)*

    _____

Exercise 3: Create your own sentences using the definitions above.

1. I can...

    Answer: <u>I can do well in school.</u>

2. I could...

    Answer: _____

3. I had better...

    Answer: _____

4. I can...

    Answer: _____

5. May I...

    Answer: _____

6. I might...

    Answer: _____

7. I ought to...

    Answer: _____

8. I have to...

    Answer: _____

9. You should...

    Answer: _____

10. I will...

    Answer: _____

11. I would...

    Answer: _____

19-2 Using *I* as the Subject for Formal Requests

Rules:	Examples:
May I or *could I* in American English is a polite and <u>formal</u> way to ask permission. *__Note:__* both are common in American English.	1. *May I* go to the bathroom? 2. *Could I* have a piece of paper?
Can I is used to <u>informally</u> ask for permission and is also common in American English.	*Can I* borrow a pencil?

19-3 Using *You* as the Subject for Formal Requests

Rules:	Examples:
Would you or *will you* is a formal way to ask a question. You use it to ask a person if he/she can perform a certain action. It is considered to be more polite than *can you* when asking a question.	1. *Would you* go to the store and buy a pound of sugar? 2. *Will you* go to the store and buy a pound of sugar?
Could you is a formal way to ask a person if it is possible for he/she to perform a specific action. It is used if you do not know if the person you are asking would want to perform the action you are requesting.	*Person 1:* **Question:** *Could you* work tomorrow? *Person 2:* **Answer:** Sure. *Notice how *person 1* does not know if *person 2* can work. *Person 1* is asking if *person 2* is available.
Can you is similar to *would you, will you,* or *could you* except for it's used informally. *Can you* is not recommended because it is not as polite as the other examples but you will hear *can you* frequently in everyday speech by Americans.	1. *Can you* go to the store? 2. *Can you* mail this letter?

19-4 Polite Request with *Would You Mind* and *Did You Mind*

Rules:	Examples:
Would you mind or *do you mind* is a polite request. It is used to describe an action that you would like to do in the future. *Would you mind* or *do you mind* is either followed by a verb ending in *-ing (gerund)* (**Example 1**) or *if* (**Example 2**).	1. *(Would/do) you mind* looking at my car? It's broken. 2. *(Would/do) you mind* if I borrowed your car?
Did you mind is used to ask permission for an action you have already done. It is always used in the past tense and is often followed by *that*.	*Did you mind* that I borrowed your car?

"Do you mind if I use your bathroom?"

Exercise

Exercise 1: Underline the correct *modal* for each sentence.

1. <u>*(Did you mind*</u> / *Can I)* that I borrowed your pencil?

2. *(Do you mind* / *May I)* go to the restroom?

3. *(Can I* / *Do you mind)* have some candy?

4. *(Would you* / *Do you mind)* go to the post office?

5. *(Do you* / *Could you)* buy my lunch? I have no money.

6. *(Can you* / *Do you)* change the TV channel?

7. *(Would you* / *can you)* mind taking these books to the library?

8. *(Can I / Do you)* mind if I watch TV?

9. *(Can I / Do you)* go to the party on Saturday?

10. *(Can I / Would you)* mind taking the trash out?

19-5 Using Imperative Sentences to Make Polite Requests

Definition:	Examples:
Imperative sentences are sentences without subjects. Imperative sentences do not use subjects because the subject in the sentence is known. *Note:* imperative sentences are used to make requests and orders.	1. *Close* the door. 2. *Open* the window. 3. *Don't* be late.

NOTICE

Wash Your Hands

DANGER

WATCH YOUR STEP

Exercise

Exercise 1: Underline the correct *verb* in each sentence that makes the most sense.

1. *(Walk / Open)* up the hill.

2. *(Go / Stop)* at the stop sign.

3. *(Mow / Play)* the lawn.

4. *(See / Walk)* faster.

5. *(Live / Open)* the door.

6. *(Drive / Grow)* slower.

7. *(See / Look)* at the time.

8. *(Write / Kick)* neater.

9. *(Carry / Run)* over there.

10. *(Swim / Dig)* into the ground.

Chapter 20
Modals (Part 2)

He *is* upset.

20-1 Expressing Degrees of Certainty

In American speech *degrees of certainty* means how confident you are about how correct a statement is.

Rules:	Examples:
If you are *100%* sure about the topic you are discussing, use *is*. *Is* is used for a statement of fact. (**Example 1**)	**1.** Tom *is* sad.
	2. Tom *must be* sad.
If you are *90%* sure about the topic you are discussing, use *must be*. (**Example 2**)	**3.** Tom *may be* sad.
	4. *Maybe* Tom's sad.
If you are *60%* sure about the topic you are discussing, use *may be, maybe, might be,* or *could be*. These words are discussing suspicious or uncertain thoughts. (**Examples 3, 4 and 5**)	**6.** Tom *might be* sad.
	7. Tom *could be* sad.

Definition:	Examples:
Must be is also used when you have complete confidence in the topic you are discussing, but you have no idea if it is completely true or completely false.	Tom is not here. He is usually in class every day. He *must be* sick. **You have no idea if Tom is truly sick or not, but you have complete confidence that he is sick.*

He *must be* rich.

Exercise

Exercise 1: Underline the correct *degree of certainty* for each sentence. Look at the percentage next to the question, then look above to match the *degree of certainty* with the percentage.

1. 60% → Terri *(could be / must be)* a girl's name.

2. 100% → My mom *(maybe / is)* a slow driver.

3. 100% → My dad *(is / must be)* sick.

4. 90% → Your shoes *(must be / is)* in the closet.

5. 100% → Tom *(must be / is)* sad.

6. 60% → John *(might be / is)* on time if he woke up early.

7. 100% → Seth *(maybe / is)* late.

8. 100% → Ann *(could be / is)* at the store.

9. 60% → Chris *(must be / maybe)* at home.

10. 90% → Your keys *(must be / are)* on the table.

20-2 Expressing Degrees of Certainty in the Negative

Degrees of certainty <u>in the negative</u> means how confident we are that a specific topic is <u>not</u> true.

Rules:	Examples:
If you are *100%* sure the topic you are discussing is <u>not</u> correct, use *is not* or *isn't*. Remember, *is* is used for a statement of fact.	1. Tom *isn't* sad. 2. Mary *isn't* slow, she just won the race.
If you are *90%* sure the topic you are discussing is <u>not</u> correct, use *could not be* or *couldn't be*. *Couldn't be* is used when you <u>believe</u> the possibility of the topic being true is very small. *Couldn't be* is also used if you are sure the topic is not true but you have no evidence to prove your opinion.	1. Seth *couldn't be* blind, he just read a magazine. 2. Seth *couldn't be* starving, he just ate lunch.
If you are **80%** sure the topic you are discussing is <u>not</u> correct, use *must not be*. Similar to *couldn't be,* you have no evidence to support your opinion. You have a strong belief. The difference between *must not be* and *couldn't* be is that you are thinking more logically when using *must be*.	**Question:** He just lost the race. I thought he was fast? **Answer:** He *must not be*.
If you are *60%* sure the topic you are discussing is <u>not</u> correct, use *may not be* or *might not be*. You are discussing suspicious or uncertain thoughts about the topic.	**Question:** I thought she was going to Harvard University? **Answer:** She *may not be*.

Exercise

Exercise 1: Underline the correct *degree of certainty* for each sentence. Look at the percentage next to the question, then look above to match the *degree of certainty* with the percentage.

1. 100% → Mike *(isn't / couldn't be)* a girl's name.

2. 60% → Tom *(must not be / may not be)* with Mary.

3. 100% → My dad *(isn't / must not be)* sick.

4. 90% → Your shoes *(are not / couldn't be)* in the closet.

5. 100% → Tom *(isn't / may not be)* sad.

6. 60% → John *(might not be / must not be)* on time if he didn't wake up early.

7. 100% → Seth *(isn't / may not be)* late.

8. 100% → Ann *(couldn't / isn't)* at the store.

9. 60% → Jake *(must not be / may not be)* at home.

10. 90% → Your keys *(isn't / must not be)* on the table.

20-3 Expressing Degrees of Certainty in the Past Tense

Degrees of certainty in the past tense means how confident we are that a specific topic was true or was not true - in the past. This means that the listener is understanding that the action you are discussing has already happened.

Past Time: Negative

Rules:	Examples:
If you are *100%* sure about the topic you are discussing, use *wasn't* or *was not*. You are *100%* sure the topic *was not* correct. **Was not** is used for a statement of fact.	1. Tom *wasn't* sad. 2. Tom *wasn't* slow; he just won the race. 3. They *were not* at the theater when we arrived.
If you are *90%* sure about the topic you are discussing, use *couldn't have been* or *could not have been*. You <u>believe</u> the possibility of the topic being true is very small.	1. Seth *couldn't have been* blind; he just read a magazine. 2. Seth *couldn't have been* starving; he just ate lunch.
If you are *80%* sure about the topic you are discussing, use *must not have been*. Similar to *couldn't have been,* you have no evidence to support your opinion. This is a strong belief. The difference between *must not have been* and *couldn't have been* is that you are more sure when using *must not have been*. **(Examples 6 and 7)**	Sarah wasn't at school <u>yesterday</u>, *she must not have* been well. **Question:** Wasn't Tom injured? **Answer:** No, Tom *was* at soccer practice last week, so he *must not have been* injured.
If you are *60%* sure about the topic you are discussing, use *may not have been* or *might not have been*. You are discussing suspicious or uncertain thoughts about the topic.	**Statement:** I don't think Sophia was sick. **Answer:** She *may not have been*.

He *couldn't have* washed his car. It's still dirty.

Past Time: Positive

Rules:	Examples:
If you are *100%* sure about the topic in the past, use *was*. You are *100%* sure the topic *was* correct. *Was* is used for a statement of fact.	**1.** Tom *was* happy. **2.** Tom *was* slow, then he practiced, and became fast.
If you are *90%* sure about the topic you are discussing, use *must have been*. You <u>believe</u> in the small possibility that the topic is true.	**1.** Sarah wasn't at school <u>yesterday</u>; she *must have been* sleeping. **2.** The dog *must have been* hungry; he ate the trash.
If you are *80%* sure about the topic you are discussing, use *could've been* or *could have been*. The difference between *must have been* and *could have been* is that you are more sure when using *must have be*.	**1.** I don't know if she was sick, but she *could've been*. **2.** I don't know if she's still at the party. She *could've* left early.
If you are *60%* sure about the topic you are discussing, use *may have been* or *might have been*. **Note:* even though your thoughts are in the present, the action still happened in the past.	**1.** Susan went home early. She *may have been* sick. **2.** The dog went through the trash. He *might have been* hungry.

She *was* younger than him.

Exercise

Exercise 1: Underline the correct *degree of certainty* for each sentence. Look at the percentage next to the question, then look above to match the *degree of certainty* with the percentage.

1. 100% → Terri (*was* / *could have been*) a girl's name.

2. 90% → My mom (*must have been* / *was*) a slow driver.

3. 80% → Your dad (*must have been* / *could have been*) sick.

4. 60% → Your shoes (*may have been* / *must have been*) in the closet.

5. 90% → Tom (*may have been* / *must have been*) sad.

6. 80% → John (*might have been* / *could have been*) on time if he woke up early.

7. 60% → Seth (*was* / *might have been*) late.

8. 100% → Ann (*must have been* / *was*) at the store.

9. 90% → Jake (*must have been* / *may have been*) at home.

10. 80% → Your keys (*could have been* / *must have been*) on the table.

20-4 Expressing Degrees of Certainty in the Future Tense

Degrees of certainty in the future tense means how confident you are that a specific topic is true or not true - in the future. This means you understand that the action(s) you are discussing <u>will</u> happen.

Future Time: Negative

Rules:	Examples:
If you are *100%* sure about the topic you are discussing, use *will not*. *Will not* is used for a statement of fact.	1. Tom *will not be* tired when he gets back from his job. 2. Tom *will not be* slow if he trains for the race.
If you are *90%* sure about the topic you are discussing, use *shouldn't* or *should not*. You believe the possibility of the topic being true is good.	1. Seth *shouldn't* do well on the exam. He did not study. 2. Seth *shouldn't be* hungry after he eats lunch.
If you are *60%* sure about the topic you are discussing, use *may not* or *might not*. You are discussing suspicious or uncertain thoughts about the topic.	1. Sarah *may not* be happy. Her dog just died. 2. Molly is not eating. She *might not be* hungry.

He *will be* learning how to fly.

Future Time: Positive

Rules:	Examples:
If you are *100%* sure about the topic you are discussing, use *will*. You are *100%* sure the topic is correct. *Will* is used for a statement of fact.	1. Tom *will be* tired when he gets back from soccer practice. 2. Tom *will be* slow if he does not practice.
If you are *90%* sure about the topic you are discussing, use *should*. You <u>believe</u> the possibility of the topic being true is good.	1. She *should be* home soon. 2. She *should* feel better tomorrow.
If you are *60%* sure about the topic you are discussing, use *may, might,* or *could*.	1. Susan *may* do 20 pushups for soccer practice. 2. The dog *might* do bad actions if you do not lock her up. 3. He *could* do great things if you give him a chance.

Exercise

Exercise 1: Underline the correct *degree of certainty* for each sentence. Look at the percentage next to the question, then look above to match the *degree of certainty* with the percentage.

1. 100% → Terri *(will be / might be)* at soccer practice.

2. 90% → She *(will not be / should not be)* at school. She's sick.

3. 100% → They *(will be / might be)* with her mother this weekend.

4. 60% → They *(will be / could be)* at the park.

5. 90% → Mike *(could be / should be)* at work.

6. 100% → John *(will be / could be)* at my house on Thursday.

7. 60% → Seth *(might not be / will not be)* on time for work. He is in traffic.

8. 100% → Ben *(will be / should be)* at the store.

9. 90% → Jake *(should be / could be)* at home by 9:00pm.

10. 80% → Your keys *(will be / might be)* on the table.

Chapter 21
Future Tenses in Time Clauses

**"*When* this tree is finished growing,
I wonder if it will grow oranges?"**

21-1 Expressing the Future Tenses in Time Clauses

Using *when, after, as soon as, before,* or *until* to discuss the time is called a *time clause*. These clauses are used to discuss future tense.

Rules:	Examples:
You do not use *will* (future tense) or *be going to* (future tense) in a time clause.	1. *When* Mike comes, please give him something to eat.
After *when, after, as soon as, before,* or *until* you need a subject and a verb. (**Example 1, 2, 3, 4 and 5**)	2. *After* we get to the park, I will give you some food.
Time clauses using the *when* time clause can start at the beginning of the sentence. (**Example 1**)	3. *As soon as* we get there, we must get our tickets.
They can also start in the middle of the sentence. (**Example 6**)	4. *Before* you go to the party, you must clean your room.
	5. *Until* I see better grades, you cannot go to your friend's house.
	6. We'll go to the store *when* we get to Ohio.

Exercise

Exercise 1: Create your own sentences using the *time clauses* above.

1. After we get to the movie theater, _I want to buy some candy._

2. When my friends come, _____

3. After we arrive, _____

4. Until you do your homework, _____

5. As soon as we get to Disney World, _____

6. After you clean the house, _____

7. Before you go to the party, _____

8. When Lucy gets here, _____

9. As soon as the plane lands, _____

10. After I go to the bank, _____

11. Before I clean the kitchen, _____

Chapter 22
Making Suggestions

"Let's **have a party?"**

22-1 Making Suggestions: *Let's, Why Don't, Shall We/I*

If you would like to suggest an action that you would like to do in the future, you can use *let's, why don't, shall we,* or *shall I*.

Rules:	Examples:
Let's always comes before the simple form of a verb. *Let's* means that you are sure about what you would like to do.	**1.** *Let's* go to the movies. **2.** *Let's* go to the park.
Why don't is a polite and formal suggestion. *Why don't* or *why doesn't* is used when you are not *100%* sure about what you would like to do and you are open to other suggestions. *Why don't* we / you / I / they *Why doesn't* she / he	**1.** *Why don't* we go to the pool? **2.** *Why don't* we go to the party?

Continued

Rules:	Examples:
Shall we / I is considered to be very polite and formal, and is not commonly used in American speech. ***Shall we / I*** is similar to ***why don't***.	1. ***Shall we*** leave at eight? 2. ***Shall I*** go to Mary's party or Maria's

"*Shall* we stay up until 12?"

Exercise

Exercise 1: Create your own sentences by *making a suggestion* for what the person/people should do in each situation.

1. Kelly is hungry.

   Answer: <u>Why don't you make some macaroni and cheese?</u>

2. Jessica can't decide whether to buy a blue car or a red car.

   Answer: _____

3. You and I need to buy our mom a present, but we don't have much money.

   Answer: _____

4. I am worried that the play will sell out.

   Answer: _____

5. Today it is going to be cold at the beach. Tomorrow, it is going to be a lot warmer.

    Answer: _____

6. Justin is too shy to ask Courtney to go on a date with him, but he really wants to.

    Answer: _____

7. Eric wants to buy a new computer, but he doesn't have any money.

    Answer: _____

8. Allison wants to work with horses when she grows up, but she is unsure of career ideas.

    Answer: _____

9. Emily needs a good book to read.

    Answer: _____

10. Missy does not understand why she failed the test.

    Answer: _____

11. I need to sell a hundred boxes of Girl Scout cookies in order to win the prize.

    Answer: _____

Chapter 23
Parallel Structure

Tom is driving the helicopter *and* john is jumping out of the helicopter.

23-1 Coordinating Conjunctions

A *coordinating conjunction* is a word or phrase used to connect other words or phrases that have the same grammatical function.

Conjunctions:	Sentence Structure:	Examples:
and	noun + *and* + noun verb + *and* + verb adjective + *and* + adjective	1. She is going to school *and* the library. 2. She is running *and* swimming. 3. Tom is both sad *and* unhappy.
but	adjective + *but* + adjective	The exercise is great *but* exhausting.

Continued

Conjunctions:	Sentence Structure:	Examples:
nor	verb + *nor* + verb	He doesn't want to read, *nor* does he want to study.
or	infinitive + *or* + infinitive	Tom wants to run **or** to lift weights for exercise.

Paired Conjunctions

Rule:	Examples:
Conjunctions can also have two conjunctions within the same sentence, connecting two ideas.	**1.** She likes reading **and** writing, **but** not speaking. **2.** Tom enjoys swimming **and** hiking, **but** not horseback riding.

Exercise

Exercise 1: Underline the correct *coordinating conjunction*. There are five questions where both answer choices are correct. There are five questions where only <u>one</u> answer choice is correct.

1. He likes to run *(and / or)* exercise.

2. My mom drives slowly *(and / but)* carefully.

3. I don't like school, *(nor / and)* do I like sports.

4. She likes to read *(and / nor)* write.

5. I like John *(and / or)* Jack.

6. I went to Oregon *(and / but)* California.

7. I saw the *Batman (and / or) Indiana Jones* movies at the same time.

8. She likes books *(and / or)* music.

9. She has a cell phone *(and / or)* a laptop.

10. Eric bought a watch *(but / and)* a pair of shoes.

Chapter 24
Negatives

"I am *not* very good with using chainsaws."

24-1 Avoiding Double Negatives

Rules:	Examples:
You cannot have <u>two</u> negative words within the same clause.	**Incorrect:** I'm *not* going to *no* party. **Correct:** I'm *not* going to the party. **Incorrect:** I *don't* have *no* money. **Correct:** I *don't* have any money.
You can have <u>two</u> negative words within the same sentence but in two different clauses.	**Correct:** I *can't* think of why he *isn't* here.

Exercise

Exercise 1: Underline the sentence that is grammatically correct?

1. A. I can't go to no game.
   B. <u>I can't go to any game.</u>

2. A. I won't have any money.
   B. I won't have no money.

3. A. I don't have no change
   B. I have no change.

4. A. She isn't going to take no shower.
   B. She isn't going to take a shower.

5. A. They didn't read no books over the summer.
   B. They didn't read any books over the summer.

6. A. Tom doesn't have no paper; you must buy your own.
   B. Tom doesn't have any paper; you must buy your own.

7. A. She doesn't have any money.
   B. She hasn't got no money.

8. A. Mike can't get no sicker.
   B. Mike can't get any sicker.

9. A. Ashley and Mike aren't not dating anymore.
   B. Ashley and Mike are not dating anymore.

10. A. I can't get no rest.
    B. I can't get any rest.

Chapter 25
Active and Passive Verb Forms

The flowers *are being sucked-up* by the vacuum.

25-1 Active and Passive Forms

Sentences can be *active* or *passive*. This means tenses also have *active forms* and *passive forms*.

Active Forms

Rule:	Examples:
Most sentences are *active*. In *active* sentences the noun performing the action is at the front of the sentence*(subject),* and the noun receiving the action is at the end of the sentence*(object).*	1. *Mike(subject)* cleans his ***room**(object).* 2. *John(subject)* reads the ***book**(object).* 3. *Karen(subject)* traveled to ***Ohio**(object).*

Sentence Structure Formula:

noun performing action + *verb* + ***noun receiving action***
Emily *answered* the ***door.***

Passive Forms

Rules:	Examples:
In *passive sentences*, the noun receiving the action is at the front of the sentence and the noun performing the action is at the end of the sentence. You can use the passive form if you think that the noun receiving the action is more important. You can also use the passive form if you do not know who is doing the action or if you do not want to talk about the noun doing the action. (**Example 3**)	1. The *room* was cleaned by *Mike*. 2. The *book* was read by *John*. 3. The *wallet* was stolen by *someone*.

Sentence Structure Formula:

noun receiving the action + be + *past participle of verb* + by + *noun doing the action*
The *car was fixed by me*.

Sample Sentences

Tenses:	Active:	Passive:
Simple Present	Once a day, *I feed* my dog.	Once a day, the dog *is fed* by Tom.
Present Continuous	Currently, Joe *is talking* to Sarah.	Currently, Sarah *is being talked* to by Joe.
Simple Past	Tom *read* the book.	The book *was read* by Tom.
Past Continuous	The maid *was cleaning* my house.	The house *was being cleaned* by the maid.
Present Perfect	The boy *has talked* to many people.	Many people *have been talked* to by the boy.
Present Perfect Continuous	Today, Tom *had been cleaning* his house for two hours before the party started.	Today, the house *had been cleaned* by Tom for two hours before the party started.

Continued

Tenses:	Active:	Passive:
Past Perfect	Susan *had cleaned* many houses before she got paid.	Many houses *had been cleaned* by Susan before she got paid.
Past Perfect Continuous	Tom *had been repairing* cars for years.	For years, cars **had been being repaired** by Tom.
Simple Future *will*	Today, we *will be washing* our car.	Today, our car *will be washed* by us.
Simple Future *be going to*	She *is going to be baking* a cake tonight.	A cake *is going to be baked* by her tonight.
Future Continuous *will*	They *will have started* the movie by the time we get to the theater.	The movie *will have started* by the time we get to the theater.
Future Continuous *be going to*	The teacher *is going to be teaching* the class.	The class *is going to be taught* by the teacher.
Future Perfect *will*	We *will have been climbing* Mount Everest for two weeks before we get to the top.	Mount Everest *will have been climbed* by us for two weeks before we get to the top.
Future Perfect *be going to*	They *are going to have to work* through the night if they are not finished in time.	The work *will have to be* completed through the night by them if they are not finished in time.
Future Perfect Continuous *will*	We *will have been cleaning* the house for ten hours before my parents arrive.	Before the arrival of my parents, *we will have been cleaning* the house for ten hours.

"I thought I *had cleaned* this closet?"

Exercise

Exercise 1: The first sentence is *active*; the second sentence is *passive*. Change the *active* to the *passive* by underlining the correct form of *be*.

1. Sophia cleans the house every day.
   Every day, the house *(is being* / *has been)* cleaned by Sophia.

2. Sophia is cleaning the house.
   The house *(is being* / *has been)* cleaned by Sophia.

3. Sophia has cleaned the house.
   The house *(is being* / *has been)* cleaned by Sophia.

4. Sophia cleaned the house.
   The house *(was* / *is)* cleaned by Sophia.

5. Sophia was cleaning the house.
   The house *(was being* / *has been)* cleaned by Sophia.

6. Sophia had cleaned the house.
   The house *(had been* / *has been)* cleaned by Sophia.

7. Sophia will clean the house.
   The house *(will be* / *is)* cleaned by Sophia.

8. Sophia is going to clean the house.
   The house *(is going to be* / *was)* cleaned by Sophia.

9. Sophia will have cleaned the house.
   The house *(will have been* / *was)* cleaned by Sophia.

Exercise 2: Read the following sentences. If they are written in active voice, write *active*, if they are written in passive voice, write *passive*.

1. I have to help my sister with her homework. _active_

2. A new leash for the dog was given by my aunt. _____

3. The National Anthem was written by Francis Scott Key. _____

4. I am sitting by the lake. _____

5. Chocolate ice cream was eaten by everyone at the party. _____

6. I stood next to the statue. _____

7. Sabrina was making everyone dinner. _____

8. The flu was passed from one classmate to another. _____

9. Tuna was fed to the cats. _____

10. The dishes were washed by Kelly. _____

Chapter 26
Real Conditionals

"If I *were* younger, I *would dance* all night."

26-1 Conditionals

Definition:	Examples:
Conditionals are sentences that discuss real and unreal situations. They are saying that you think an action will happen if another action happens. They also suggest ideas about a topic. There are two kinds of conditional sentences: *real* and *unreal*. *Real conditional sentences* describe real-life situations. (**Examples 1 and 2**) *Unreal conditional sentences* describe unreal, imaginary situations. (**Examples 3 and 4**)	1. If the weather is too hot, we will not go to the beach. (***real, not imaginary***) 2. My mom always cooked when I was younger. (***real, not imaginary***) 3. If I could fly, I would go to California. (***unreal, imaginary***) 4. If I had I million dollars, I would buy my own island. (***unreal, imaginary***)

*"**When** I see a copy machine, I like to copy my face."*

26-2 Present Real Conditionals

Rules:	Examples:
The *present real conditional* is used to express your <u>normal</u> actions in <u>real</u> situations. Both *if* and **when** are used with the present real conditional. Using *if* suggests that something happens less frequently. Using **when** suggests that something happens regularly.	1. ***When*** I *go* to the movies, I ***like*** to buy popcorn. 2. ***If*** it ***rains,*** I ***take*** an umbrella. 3. ***When*** I *go* to the store, I ***buy*** food.

Sentence Structure Formula:

if / when + *simple present, simple present*

1. ***If*** I *exercise*, my heart *is* stronger.
2. ***When*** I *fly* in an airplane, I *get* sick.

simple present + *if / when simple present*

1. My heart *is* stronger, ***if*** I *exercise*.
2. I *get* sick, **when** I *fly* in an airplane.

Note: You do not need to use *I* in your sentences to use conditional. You can use *he / she / it / they / Tom / Emily / etc.*

"*When* I get my paycheck, I'm going to New York City!"

Exercise

Exercise 1: Underline the correct form of *present tense* for the *conditional clauses*.

1. If I *(walk / walked / will walk)* to school, I usually *(take / took / will take)* the bus.

2. If I *(go / will go / went)* to school, I usually *(took / take / will take)* usually the bus.

3. If I *(drank / drink / will drink)* too much water, I have to *(go / will go / went)* to the bathroom.

4. If the dog *(bit / bites / bited)* a person, he has to *(go / will go / went)* to the animal shelter.

5. When I *(washed / wash / will wash)* my car, I usually *(scrubbed / scrub / will scrub)* the tires.

6. When Tom and Pat *(travel / will travel / traveled)* to California, they usually *(go / went / will go)* to Los Angles.

7. When the city of New York *(has / have / will have)* a parade, the city *(closed / close / will close)* the streets.

8. If I *(fail / failed / will fail)* this test, I *(start / started / will start)* crying.

9. When I *(walked / will walk / walk)* to the store, I usually *(walked / will walk / walk)* on the sidewalk.

10. If I don't *(do / doing / done)* my homework, my mother usually *(yell / yells / yelling)* at me.

26-3 Past Real Conditionals

Rules:	Examples:
Past real conditional is used when an action occurred in the past, and you chose to do a second action in the past because of the result of the first action. (**Example 1**)	1. When I ***was*** in school, I ***used to play*** sports.
	2. ***If*** I ***were*** in school, I ***would have studied*** a lot.
Remember, past real conditional is in the past.	
	3. When I ***was*** younger, I ***used to*** read picture books.
Look at the phrase ***used to*** in example 1. ***Used to*** tells the listener that you did an action in the past but you no longer do the action in the present. ***Used to*** is used to help the listener understand that your action was a habit (an action that you did many times).	4. ***If*** I ***were*** younger, I ***would have*** studied more.
Look at the phrase ***would have*** in example 2. ***Would have*** tells the listener that you were thinking about doing an action in the past, but you decided not to.	
Both ***if*** and ***when*** are used in the past real conditional. Use ***if*** when you are telling the listener that an action did not happen regularly. Use ***when*** to tell the listener that an action happened regularly.	
Note: The phrase ***would have*** is typically used with ***if***. (**Example 2**)	

Sentence Structure Formula:

if / when + *simple past, simple past*

1. ***If*** *were* smarter, I would have *read* more books.
2. ***When*** I *spoke* to people in large groups, I *used* to be nervous.

simple past + ***if / when*** *simple past*

1. I would have *read* more books, ***if*** *were* smarter.
2. I *used* to be nervous, ***when*** I *spoke* to people in large groups.

Note: You do not need to use ***I*** in your sentences to use conditional. You can use ***he / she / it / they / Tom / Emily / etc.***

"If we *were* smarter, we *would have worn* raincoats"

Exercise

Exercise 1: Underline the correct *verb* for the *past real conditional.*

1. When I *(had / have / will have)* a dollar, I used to *(spend / spent / will spend)* it. Now, I put the money in a savings bank account.

2. If I *(read / red / will read)* a long book in English, it used to *(be / been / will be)* difficult. Now, with practice, it's much easier.

3. When I *(had / have / will have)* to mow the grass, it usually *(took / take / will took)* me a long time. Now, I hire a person to cut the grass.

4. If I *(run / ran / will run)* I a long distance, I usually *(took / take / will took)* a long time. Now, I can run marathon.

5. If the weather *(is / was / were)* good, I usually *(took / take / will took)* my dog on a walk.

6. When I *(had / have / will have)* to complete my school work, I often *(forget / forgot / forgotten)*. Now, I am older and wiser.

7. When I *(had / have / will have)* an argument with my mother, I usually *(get / got / gotten)* upset. Now, I don't anymore.

8. I used to *(walk / walked / will walk)* to work every day. Now I drive.

9. When I was younger and I *(get / got / gotten)* invited to many parties, I usually *(took / take / will took)* a bottle of wine with me.

10. I used to *(drink / drank / will drink)* a lot, but now I don't *(drink / drank / will drink)* alcohol anymore.

"*If* I look for a new job tonight, *I will* be happier tomorrow."

26-4 Future Real Conditionals

Rules:	Examples:
The *future real conditional* describes what you think you will do in the future after another action occurs. (**Example 1**)	1. **When** I *run* the marathon tomorrow, I **will** be tired when I finish.
It is different from other real conditional forms because you do not know what will happen in the future. You must guess.	2. **If** I *study* English, I **will** be fluent.
	3. **When** Tom *travels* to France, he **will** take a plane.
Both **if** and **when** are used with the future real conditional. Using **if** says that you do not know if an action will happen or not. **When** says that an action will happen, but you are waiting for that action to occur. (**Examples 2 and 3**)	*Remember: When* is *100%* - you are sure the action will happen.
	Remember: If is *50%* - you are not sure an action will happen.

Sentence Structure Formula:

If / When + *simple present, simple future.*

1. **If** Tom *takes* that job, he *will have* to move.
2. **When** Lucy *goes* to the beach, she *will have* to use sunscreen.

simple future + *if / when* + *simple present.*

1. I *will cook* dinner, **if** you *wash* the dishes.
2. Jack *will walk* the dog, **if** you *feed* him.

Note: You do not need to use *I* in your sentences. You can use *he / she / it / they / Tom / Emily / etc.*

"*If* I take the stairs, *it will* take me longer."

Exercise

Exercise 1: Underline the correct form of *future real conditional* for each sentence.

1. If I *(go / gone / will go)* to the gym tonight, I *(will need / will needed / needed)* a towel to go swimming.

2. If I *(drive / will drive / will drove)* to the store now, I *(miss / missed / will miss)* will my favorite television show.

3. When I *(got / get / will got)* some money, I'm *(will buy /going to buy / bought)* a new computer.

4. When the weather *(get / gets / got)* better, we will *(start / started / starting)* going to the beach.

5. If I can *(complete / completing / completed)* my homework, I'm *(go / gone / going)* to the park.

6. If I *(drive / drove / driving)* to California, I'm *(going / going / gone)* to take my wife with me.

7. When I *(go / going / gone)* to the movie theater, I will (buy / buying / bought) some candy.

8. If she does her *(work / working / worked)* poorly, I will have to *(ask / asking / asked)* her to do the work again.

9. If the book *(are / is)* too long, I will not *(has / had / have)* a chance to finish it.

10. When I get *(work / working / worked)* to this morning, I am *(go / going / gone)* to call my mother.

Chapter 27
Unreal Conditionals

"*If* I *were* smarter, this job *would be* easier."

27-1 Present Unreal Conditionals

Rules:	Examples:
Same as real conditional sentences, *unreal conditional* sentences are saying that you think an action will happen if another action happens.	**1. *If* I *were* rich, I *would fly* to the moon.**
	2. *If* I *were* taller, I *would play* professional basketball.
The *present unreal conditional* is used to talk about your actions in <u>unreal</u> situations. These situations are imaginary actions.	**3. *If* I *were* a better repairperson, I *would fix* my broken computer.**
In the present unreal conditional, always use *if* and *were*.	
*Note: When you are discussing imaginary situations ***when*** cannot be used.	

Sentence Structure Formula:

if + simple past, **would** + simple present

1. If I *were* rich, I **would** *fly* to the moon.
2. If you *were* nicer, I **would** *help* you.

would + simple present, *if* + simple past

1. I **would** *fly* to the moon, **if** I *were* rich.
2. I **would** *help* you, **if** you *were* nicer.

Note: You do not need to use *I* in your sentences to use conditional. You can use *he / she / it / they / Tom / Emily / etc.*

"*If* we *were* less busy, we *would go* on vacation."

Exercise

Exercise 1: Underline the correct form of the *present unreal conditional*. Follow the sentence structure above to help you answer the questions.

1. If I *(start / started / will start)* working, I would *(buy / bought /will buy)* a car.

2. Tom would *(walk / walked / will walk)* if he hadn't *(break / broken / will break)* his leg.

3. If Ana *(begun / begin / will begin)* reading, she would *(been / be / will be)* better at English.

4. If the teacher *(grade / graded / will grade)* my test, I would know what grade I *(get / got / will got)* in my class.

5. If I *(go / went / will go)* to the movies, I would not *(do / will do / done)* well on my test.

Exercise 2: Underline the correct form of the *present unreal conditional*. Follow the sentence structure above to help you answer the questions.

1. **Question:** Who would you *(pick / picked / will pick)* if you *(go / will go / went)* to the school dance?

   Answer: I *(would pick / picked / will pick)* Ann or Emily.

2. **Question:** What would you *(buy / will buy / bought)* if you *(have / had / will have)* one million dollars?

   Answer: I would *(buy / will buy / bought)* a big house.

3. **Question:** What would you *(done / will do / do)* if your wallet *(were / was)* stolen?

   Answer: I would *(call / called / will call)* the police.

4. **Question:** Where would *(live / lived / will live)* if you came to the United States?

   Answer: I would *(live / lived / will live)* in Washington, DC.

5. **Question:** What car would you *(bought / buy / will buy)* if you could *(bought / buy / will buy)* any car in the world?

   Answer: I would *(bought / buy / will buy)* a Porsche.

27-2 Past Unreal Conditionals

Rules:	Examples:
The *past unreal conditional* is used to express imaginary or unreal situations in the past. You are describing an action you *would have* done differently or how an action *could have* happened differently. (**Example 1**) *Note:* the past unreal conditional is in the past, so you no longer do the actions in the present. Only the word *if* is used with the past unreal conditional. When you are discussing imaginary situations **when** cannot be used.	1. *If* I *had been* a better student, I *could have earned* better grades. 2. *If* I *would have played* the lottery <u>last week</u>, I *could have won* $100 million. 3. *If* I *had been* faster, I *could have been* an Olympian.

Sentence Structure Formula:

If + *past perfect*, ***would/could have*** + *past participle*

1. *If* I *had been* a famous scientist, I ***could have*** been rich.
2. *If* you *had been* listening, you ***would have*** heard the directions.

would/could have + *past participle*, *if* + *past perfect*

1. I ***could have*** been rich, *if* I *had been* a famous scientist.
2. You ***would have*** heard the directions, *if* you *had been* listening.

Noun + ***would have*** + *past participle*, *if* + *past perfect*

1. Susan ***would have*** studied, *if* she had not *gone* to work.
2. I ***could have*** helped, *if* you had *asked* me.

Noun + ***would have*** + *past participle*, *if* + *past perfect*

1. *If* she had not *gone* to work, Susan ***would have*** studied.
2. *If* you had *asked* me, I ***could have*** helped.

Note: You do not need to use *I* in your sentences to use conditional. You can use ***he / she / it / they / Tom / Emily / etc.***

"If I *had downloaded* another game, I *would have been* much happier."

Exercise

Exercise 1: Underline the correct *past unreal conditional* form for each sentence.

1. If I had *(be / been / being)* smarter, I could have *(be / been / being)* accepted into Harvard.

2. If she had *(be / been / being)* faster, I would have *(give / giving / given)* her a better tip.

3. I would have *(mow / mowing / mowed)* the lawn quicker, if we *(have / had / having)* a better lawn mower.

4. Seth could have *(win / winning / won)* the race if he had *(practice / practiced / practicing)* more.

5. Susan would have *(move / moving / moved),* if she had *(find / found / finding)* a nice house.

6. If Mary would have *(work / worked / working)* hard, she might still *(have / had / having)* her job.

7. If Michael had been *(pay / paying / paid)* attention, he would have *(get / got / gotten)* a better grade on the test.

8. Ann would have *(travel / traveling / traveled)* to Paris if she could have *(afford / affording / afforded)* the plane ticket.

9. I would have *(drive / driven / drove)* to California, if gas had not *(be / been / being)* so expensive.

10. I could have *(be / been / being)* a famous musician if I would have *(win / winning / won)* the contest.

"If we were not so dizzy, I would drive home."

27-3 Future Unreal Conditionals

Rules:	Examples:
The *future unreal conditional* is used to describe imaginary actions you think you will do in the future.	1. *If* I did not have to work <u>next year</u>, I *would spend* all year traveling the world.
Future unreal conditional is different from other unreal conditional forms because you do not know what will happen in the future. You must guess.	2. *If* I had money, I *would quit* my job <u>tomorrow</u>. 3. *If* I were moving to London <u>next year</u>, I *would have* a going-away party.
It is called <u>unreal</u> because it is not likely or possible the action will happen in the future.	
Only *if* is used with future unreal conditional. Using *if* says that you do not know if an action will happen or not. You must guess. Using *when* says that an action will definitely happen in the future.	

Sentence Structure Formula:

If + *simple past, would* + *simple present.*

1. *If* I *had* a million dollars, I *would fly* to the moon.
2. *If* I *were* a king, I *would be* rich.

would + *simple present,* *if* + *simple past.*

1. I *would fly* to the moon, *If* I *had* a million dollars,
2. I *would be* rich, *If* I *were* a king.

Note: You do not need to use *I* in your sentences to use conditional. You can use *he / she / it / they / Tom / Emily / etc.*

"*If I* were not so cheap, I *would call* a professional this afternoon."

Exercise

Exercise 1: Underline the correct *future unreal conditional* form for each sentence.

1. If I *(has / had / have)* a good car, I would not have to worry about fixing it every day.

2. I would *(go / going / gone)* to New York right now, if I were on vacation.

3. If I were rich, I would be *(travel / traveled / traveling)* the world.

4. If I *(has / had / have)* a child, I would be a great parent.

5. If I were *(go / going / gone)* to California, it would be wonderful.

6. If I were not going to work, I would be *(travel / traveled / traveling)* to the beach.

7. If I had a good computer, I could *(complete / completed / completing)* my work faster.

8. I would *(go / going / gone)* to work today, if I wasn't sick.

9. If I were a famous actor, I would be *(live / lived / living)* in Hollywood.

10. If I were *(move / moved / moving)* to Washington, DC, my wife would be going with me.

Chapter 28
Complex Conditionals

He is *running* a relay race.

28-1 Continuous Conditionals

Definition:	Examples:
The *continuous conditional* is an action that continues for a length of time. (**Example 1**)	1. He is <u>running</u> a marathon. *<u>Running</u> is the continuous verb.*
You should know the continuous verbs (progressive tense) from the previous chapters.	2. *If I were* <u>running</u> a marathon, I *would* be practicing today. *<u>Running</u> is the continuous verb.*
Conditional + Continuous is used to discuss unreal or imaginary situations that continue for a length of time.	3. *If I were* <u>moving</u> to Nepal, I *would* have a going away party. *<u>Moving</u> is the continuous verb.*
Note: it is called <u>unreal</u> because it is not likely or possible the action will happen.	

Rules:	Examples:
Present Unreal Conditional + Continuous: *Present unreal conditional + continuous* is used to discuss imaginary or unreal actions that could be currently happening.	**1.** If the teacher is ***still teaching***, I ***would raise*** my hand and ask a question. **2.** If the janitor is ***still cleaning***, I ***would ask*** him to empty your garbage can.
Past Unreal Conditional + Continuous: *Past unreal conditional + continuous* is used to discuss imaginary or unreal actions happening in the past.	**1.** If I ***had been*** at the party, I ***would have seen*** the girl I liked. **2.** If he ***had been*** studying, he ***would have passed*** the test.
Future Unreal Conditional + Continuous: *Future unreal conditional + continuous* is used to discuss imaginary or unreal actions happening in the future.	**1.** If I ***were going*** to the concert <u>tomorrow</u>, I ***would*** not be sad. **2.** If I ***were running*** in the race <u>tomorrow</u>, I ***would*** go and practice this afternoon.

"If I *had been* exercising, I *would not have gotten* so out-of-shape."

Exercise

Exercise 1: Underline the correct *continuous conditional* form for each sentence.

1. She is *(drive / <u>driving</u> / will drive)* down the street.

2. If Ann is still *(watch / watched / watching)* television, I would *(ask / asked / asking)* her to help you.

3. If Tom is *(do / doing / done)* his homework, I would *(ask / asked / asking)* him to help you with yours.

4. If Jennifer is *(practice / practiced / practicing)* for the marathon, I would *(practice / practiced / practicing)* with her.

5. If she had been *(pay / paid / paying)* attention in class, she would *(have / has / had)* gotten an "A" on her test.

6. If the dog *(have / has / had)* been at home, he could have *(stop / stopped / stopping)* the thief from coming in the house.

7. If Mike had been *(listen / listened / listening),* he would have *(hear / hearing / heard)* the teacher give the directions.

8. If I were *(study / studying / studied)* English in the United States, I would *(quit / quitting)* my job tomorrow.

9. If I were *(make / making / made)* a lot of money, I would *(buy / buying / bought)* a big house for my family and myself.

   If I were *(speak / speaking / spoken)* English, I would try and *(ask / asked / asking)* my boss for more money.

28-2 Mixed Conditionals

Sometimes *unreal conditional* sentences are mixed. Study the examples below to learn how to mix conditional verb forms.

Present Unreal Conditional	Past Unreal Conditional
1. If I *were* smarter, →	I *would have gotten* a job as an astronaut.
2. If she *were* a doctor, →	she *would have prescribed* you medicine.

Present Unreal Conditional	Future Unreal Conditional
1. If I *spoke* French, →	I *would move* to Paris.
2. If I could *understand* English, →	I *would move* to New York.

Future Unreal Conditional	Past Unreal Conditional
1. If I *weren't starting* school in the fall, →	I *would have taken* that new job.
2. If we *weren't going to be* parents in a couple of months, →	I *would have spent* all my extra money on luxury items.

Future Unreal Conditional	Present Unreal Conditional
1. If I *weren't working* this Summer, →	I *would learn* how to play soccer.
2. If I *were going to* Brussels this fall, →	I *would be* excited.

Past Unreal Conditional	Present Unreal Conditional
1. If I *had started* math sooner, →	I *would be* an accountant.
2. If I *had studied* harder in school, →	I *would be* making more money.

Continued

Past Unreal Conditional	Future Unreal Conditional
1. If Tom *had completed* his homework, →	he **would be** going to the party.
2. If she *had studied* for the exam, →	she **would be** going to a better school this Fall.

"If I *weren't going* to work today, I *would go* to the doctor."

Exercise

Exercise 1: Underline the correct *mixed conditional* for each sentence.

1. If I *(was / were / am)* more athletic, I would be a marathon runner.

2. If I had *(finish / finished / finishing)* the book, I would be going to the book discussion tonight.

3. If I *(aren't / weren't / am)* running the marathon this Fall, I would have eaten more desserts at dinner.

4. If you were bilingual*, I would *(send / sent / sended)* you to the conference in New York City.

5. If I *(was practiced / had practiced / am practiced)* longer, I would be a lot better at playing my guitar.

6. If I weren't leaving for Paris, I would have *(buyed / bought / buy)* that apartment.

7. If I weren't driving to my parents' house this weekend, I *(would work / would worked / were work)* on my project for school.

8. If I had *(drink / drank / drunk)* that spoiled milk, I would be very sick now.

9. If they weren't talking so much, they *(would have here / would have hear / would have heard)* the directions.

10. If they had stopped at the stoplight, they would not be *(ask / asked / asking)* the police officer for forgiveness.

The ability to speak two languages.

"If I were to leave now, maybe my boss will not see this."

28-3 *Were to* Conditionals - Present, Past and Future

Rules:	Examples:
Were to can be used in the <u>present</u> to emphasize that the conditional form is <u>extremely</u> unlikely. The *were to* form is only used in the if-clause.	If I *were to have* one million dollars, it would be much easier to do my homework.
Were to can be used in the <u>past</u> to emphasize that the conditional form is <u>extremely</u> unlikely. The *were to* form is only used in the if-clause.	If you *were to have suffered* from a heart attack, this family would not do well without you.
Were to can be used in the <u>future</u> to emphasize that the conditional form is <u>extremely</u> unlikely. The *were to* form is only used in the if-clause.	If I *were to win* the lottery *next month*, I would definitely quite my job *tomorrow*.

Continued

Sentence Structure Formula:

If I *were to* + verb(present) + *would* + verb(present)
If I *were to study* now, I *would* not have to study tonight.

If I *were to* have + (verb)past + would + (verb)past
If you *were to* have *studied*, I *would* have *done* better on the test.

If I *were to* + verb + would/will + verb(present)
If I *were to* study *tomorrow night*, I *will* not have study *tomorrow*.

**"If I *were to* finish tonight,
I *will* go to the beach in the morning."**

Exercise

Exercise 1: Underline the correct *verb* form for each *were to conditional* sentence.

1. If I were to (*see* / *saw* / *seen*) a ghost, I would be so scared.

2. If the tornado were to have (*destroy* / *destroying* / *destroyed*) the school, the people of the city would be very upset.

3. If I were to (*get* / *got* / *gotten*) an "A" on my test, my mom will allow me to out with my friends tonight.

4. If someone were to (*has* / *have* / *had*) nice car we could borrow, tonight would be perfect.

5. If the computer were to (*broke, break* / *broken*) down, I would lose all of my work.

6. If my cell phone were to *(go / going /gone)* off in the middle of the exam, I would be so embarrassed.

7. If we were to *(has / have / had)* an earthquake, the city would be in panic.

8. Question: Did you study for the test tomorrow?

   Answer: No, but if I were to *(study / studying / studied)* tonight, for the whole test, I may pass.

9. If I were to *(pass / passing / passed)* my driving test tomorrow, I will finally have my driver's license.

10. If I were to *(cook / cooking / cooked)* you dinner tonight, you must wash the dishes.

References

List of Irregular Verbs

Base Form →	Simple Past Tense →	Past Participle
awake	awoke	awoken
be	was, were	been
bear	bore	born
beat	beat	beat
become	became	become
begin	began	begun
bend	bent	bent
beset	beset	beset
bet	bet	bet
bid	bid/bade	bid/bidden
bind	bound	bound
bite	bit	bitten
bleed	bled	bled
blow	blew	blown
break	broke	broken
breed	bred	bred
bring	brought	brought
broadcast	broadcast	broadcast
build	built	built
burn	burned/burnt	burned/burnt
burst	burst	burst
buy	bought	bought
cast	cast	cast
catch	caught	caught
choose	chose	chosen
cling	clung	clung
come	came	come
cost	cost	cost
creep	crept	crept
cut	cut	cut
deal	dealt	dealt
dig	dug	dug
dive	dived/dove	dived
do	did	done
draw	drew	drawn
dream	dreamed/dreamt	dreamed/dreamt
drive	drove	driven
drink	drank	drunk
eat	ate	eaten
fall	fell	fallen
feed	fed	fed

feel	felt	felt
fight	fought	fought
find	found	found
fit	fit	fit
flee	fled	fled
fling	flung	flung
fly	flew	flown
forbid	forbade	forbidden
forget	forgot	forgotten
forego (forgo)	forewent	foregone
forgive	forgave	forgiven
forsake	forsook	forsaken
freeze	froze	frozen
get	got	gotten
give	gave	given
go	went	gone
grind	ground	ground
grow	grew	grown
hang	hung	hung
hear	heard	heard
hide	hid	hidden
hit	hit	hit
hold	held	held
hurt	hurt	hurt
keep	kept	kept
kneel	knelt	knelt
knit	knit	knit
know	knew	know
lay	laid	laid
lead	led	led
leap	leaped/leapt	leaped/leapt
learn	learned/learnt	learned/learnt
leave	left	left
lend	lent	lent
let	let	let
lie	lay	lain
light	lighted/lit	lighted
lose	lost	lost
make	made	made
mean	meant	meant
meet	met	met
misspell	misspelled/misspelt	misspelled/misspelt
mistake	mistook	mistaken
mow	mowed	mowed/mown
overcome	overcame	overcome
overdo	overdid	overdone
overtake	overtook	overtaken

overthrow	overthrew	overthrown
pay	paid	paid
plead	pled	pled
prove	proved	proved/proven
put	put	put
quit	quit	quit
read	read	read
rid	rid	rid
ride	rode	ridden
ring	rang	rung
rise	rose	risen
run	ran	run
saw	sawed	sawed/sawn
say	said	said
see	saw	seen
seek	sought	sought
sell	sold	sold
send	sent	sent
set	set	set
sew	sewed	sewed/sewn
shake	shook	shaken
shave	shaved	shaved/shaven
shear	shore	shorn
shed	shed	shed
shine	shone	shone
shoe	shoed	shoed/shod
shoot	shot	shot
show	showed	showed/shown
shrink	shrank	shrunk
shut	shut	shut
sing	sang	sung
sink	sank	sunk
sit	sat	sat
sleep	slept	slept
slay	slew	slain
slide	slid	slid
sling	slung	slung
slit	slit	slit
smite	smote	smitten
sow	sowed	sowed/sown
speak	spoke	spoken
speed	sped	sped
spend	spent	spent
spill	spilled/spilt	spilled/spilt
spin	spun	spun
spit	spit/spat	spit
split	split	split

spread	spread	spread
spring	sprang/sprung	sprung
stand	stood	stood
steal	stole	stolen
stick	stuck	stuck
sting	stung	stung
stink	stank	stunk
stride	strode	stridden
strike	struck	struck
string	strung	strung
strive	strove	striven
swear	swore	sworn
sweep	swept	swept
swell	swelled	swelled/swollen
swim	swam	swum
swing	swung	swung
take	took	taken
teach	taught	taught
tear	tore	torn
tell	told	told
think	thought	thought
thrive	thrived/throve	thrived
throw	threw	thrown
thrust	thrust	thrust
tread	trod	trodden
understand	understood	understood
uphold	upheld	upheld
upset	upset	upset
wake	woke	woken
wear	wore	worn
weave	weaved/wove	weaved/woven
wed	wed	wed
weep	wept	wept
wind	wound	wound
win	won	won
withhold	withheld	withheld
withstand	withstood	withstood
wring	wrung	wrung
write	wrote	written

Compound Nouns List

A

abovementioned
aforementioned
afterbirth
afterburner
aftermath
airbrush
aircraft
airfield
airliner
airmail
airman
airport
airship
anybody
anymore
anyone
applesauce
armchair
armpit
arrowhead
authorship

B

backbite
backdrop
backfield
backfire
background
backhand
backlash
backlog
backside
backslide
backspin
backstop
backstretch
backstroke
backtrack
backward
backwash
backwater
backwoods

bagpipe
ballroom
bandwagon
bankbook
bankroll
barnstorm
barnyard
barroom
bartender
baseball
baseboard
bathroom
beachcomber
beachhead
bedridden
bedrock
bedroll
bedspread
bedtime
beehive
beeline
bellbottom
bellhop
billboard
billfold
blackbird
blackboard
blacklist
blackmail
blacktop
blockbuster
bloodsucker
blueberry
bluebird
blueblood
bluegrass
bobcat
bobtail
bookmobile
bookworm
boxcar
brainstorm
brainwash
breadwinner
breakfast

breakup
brickbat
bridegroom
bridgehead
briefcase
broadcast
brotherhood
buckshot
buckskin
bucktooth
bugbear
bulldog
bulldozer
bullfight
bullfrog
bullheaded
bullpen
buttercup
butterfingers
butterfly
buttermilk
bygone
bypass
byword

C

capsize
caretaker
carhop
carport
carsick
catfish
catnip
cattail
chairman
chalkboard
championship
cheapskate
checkmate
checkroom
checkup
cheesecloth
chestnut
chickpea

chickweed
chopstick
citizenship
clapboard
claptrap
classmate
clockwise
clockwork
clodhopper
clotheshorse
cobweb
copycat
copyreader
copyright
copywriter
corkscrew
cornerstone
cornstalk
cottonmouth
cottontail
cottonwood
countdown
counterattack
counterbalance
counterclockwise
countermeasure
counteroffensive
counterpane
counterpart
counterpoint
counterpoise
counterrevolution
countersign
countersink
countertenor
counterweight
countryside
courthouse
courtship
courtyard
cowbird
cowboy
cowcatcher
cowhide
cowlick

cowpoke
cowpox
cowpuncher
cowslip
crabgrass
crackdown
crackerjack
crackpot
crackup
cradlesong
crankcase
crankshaft
crapshooter
crawfish
crestfallen
crossbar
crossbeam
crossbones
crossbow
crossbreed
crosscurrent
crosscut
crosspiece
crossroad
crosstalk
crosswalk
crosswise
crowbar
crybaby
cubbyhole
cupboard
cupcake
cutback
cutlass
cutlet
cutoff
cutthroat
cutup

D

daredevil
darkroom
dashboard
dateline
daybreak
daydream
dayflower

daylight
daylights
daytime
deadbeat
deadline
deadlock
deadwood
deathbed
deathblow
deathwatch
dimwit
dishcloth
dishwasher
doeskin
dogcatcher
dogfight
dogfish
doghouse
dogtrot
dogwood
doorbell
doorknob
doorman
doormat
doorway
doughboy
doughnut
dovetail
downcast
downfall
downgrade
downhearted
downhill
downpour
downright
downstairs
downstream
downtown
downtrodden
downward
downwind
dragnet
drainpipe
drawback
drawbridge
drawstring
dressmaker

driftwood
driveway
dropout
drugstore
drumstick
duckbill
duckboard
duckpin
dugout
dumbbell
dumbwaiter
dustpan

E

earache
eardrum
earflap
earmark
earmuff
earphone
earring
earshot
earthquake
earthwork
earthworm
earwax
earwig
eastward
eavesdrop
egghead
eggnog
eggplant
elbowroom
elderberry
elsewhere
enamelware
endless
endmost
endplate
evergreen
evermore
everyday
everything
eyeball
eyebrow
eyeglass
eyelash

eyelet
eyelid
eyepiece
eyesight
eyesore
eyestrain
eyetooth
eyewitness

F

fairground
fairway
fallout
falsehood
fancywork
fanfare
fanlight
farewell
farmhouse
farmyard
farseeing
fatback
fatherhood
featherbed
featherweight
feedback
fellowship
fiberboard
fiddlesticks
figurehead
filmgoer
fingerboard
fingernail
fingerprint
firearm
fireball
firebrand
firebug
firecracker
firedamp
firefly
fireman
fireplace
fireplug
fireproof
fireside
firetrap

firewood
firework
fishbowl
fisherman
fishhook
fishwife
flagpole
flagship
flagstaff
flagstone
flameout
flapjack
flashback
flashlight
flatboat
flatcar
flatfish
flatfoot
flatiron
flatware
flintlock
floodgate
floodlight
floorwalker
flophouse
flyblown
flyby
flycatcher
flyleaf
flypaper
flyspeck
flyweight
flywheel
foghorn
folklore
foodstuff
foolhardy
foolproof
football
footboard
footbridge
footfall
foothill
foothold
footlights
footlocker
footloose

footman
footnote
footpath
footprint
footrest
footstep
footstool
footwear
footwork
forbear
forearm
forebear
forecast
forecastle
foreclose
forefather
forefinger
forefoot
forefront
forego
foregone
foreground
forehand
foreleg
forelimb
forelock
foreman
foremast
foremost
forenoon
foreordain
forequarter
forerunner
foresail
foresee
foreshadow
foreshore
foreshorten
foresight
forestall
foretaste
foretell
forethought
forewarn
foreword
formfitting
fortnight

fountainhead
fourscore
foursome
foursquare
fourteen
foxglove
foxhole
framework
freebooter
freedman
freehand
freehold
freeman
freestanding
freestone
freethinker
freeway
freshman
freshwater
fretwork
frogman
frostbite
fruitcake
fullback

G

gainsay
gallstone
gamecock
gamesome
gangplank
gangway
gaslight
gasworks
gatecrasher
gatekeeper
gateway
gearbox
gearshift
gemstone
gentleman
ghostwriter
gingerbread
giveaway
globetrotter
glowworm
goalkeeper

goatskin
godfather
godmother
goldbrick
goldenrod
goldfish
goldsmith
gooseberry
grandchild
granddaughter
grandfather
grandma
grandmother
grandpa
grandparent
grandson
grandstand
grapefruit
grapeshot
grapevine
grasshopper
grassland
grassroots
gravestone
graveyard
greenback
greenhorn
greenhouse
greenwood
greyhound
griddlecake
gridiron
grillroom
grindstone
groundwork
grubstake
guardhouse
guardsman
guesswork
guidebook
guideline
guidepost
gumdrop
gumshoe
gunboat
guncotton
gunfire

gunlock
gunman
gunpowder
gunshot
gunsmith
guttersnipe

H

hacksaw
haddock
hailstone
hairbreadth
hairbrush
haircloth
haircut
hairdo
hairdresser
hairline
hairpin
hairsbreadth
hairsplitting
hairspring
halfback
half-breed
halfhearted
halfway
hallway
hammerhead
hamstring
handbag
handball
handbill
handbook
handcar
handcart
handclasp
handcuff
handmade
handmaid
handout
handpick
handrail
handshake
handsome
handspring
handwriting
handyman

hangdog
hangman
hangnail
hangout
hangover
hardheaded
hardhearted
hardpan
hardship
hardtack
hardtop
hardware
hardwood
harebrained
harelip
hatchway
haycock
hayfork
hayloft
haymow
hayseed
haystack
haywire
hazelnut
headache
headband
headdress
headfirst
headgear
headland
headlight
headline
headlock
headlong
headmaster
headmistress
headphone
headquarters
headrest
headset
headstall
headstone
headstrong
headwaiter
headwaters
headway
hearsay

heartache
heartbeat
heartbreak
heartburn
hearthstone
heartsick
heartstrings
heavyset
heavyweight
hedgehog
hedgehop
heirloom
hellcat
hellhole
helpmate
helpmeet
hemstitch
henceforth
henchman
henpeck
hereabout
hereafter
hereby
herein
hereof
hereon
hereto
heretofore
hereunto
hereupon
herewith
herringbone
herself
heyday
hideaway
hidebound
highball
highborn
highboy
highbred
highbrow
highhanded
highland
highlander
highlands
highlight
highroad

highway
highwayman
hijack
hillbilly
hillside
hilltop
hindmost
hindquarter
hindsight
hinterland
hobbyhorse
hobnail
hoecake
hogshead
hogwash
holdup
hollyhock
homebody
homecoming
homeland
homemade
homemaker
homeroom
homesick
homespun
homestead
homestretch
homeward
homework
honeybee
honeycomb
honeydew
honeymoon
hoodwink
hookup
hookworm
hopscotch
horseback
horseflesh
horseflies
horsehair
horsehide
horselaugh
horseman
horsemanship
horseplay
horsepower

horseradish
horseshoe
hotbed
hotheaded
hothouse
hotshot
hourglass
houseboat
housebreaking
housecoat
houseflies
household
househusband
housekeeper
housewarming
housewife
housework
hovercraft
however
huckleberry
humankind
humbug
humdinger
humdrum
hummingbird
humpback
hunchback
huntsman
husbandman
hushpuppy

I

iceberg
icebound
iceboxes
icebreaker
ideal
inchworm
income
indoors
infield
infuse
infusion
inhale
inkblot
inkwell
inland

inmate
inpatient
inroad
inset
inside
insole
install
instep
invest
invoice
inward
ironbound
ironclad
ironware
ironwork
ironworks
itself

J

jackass
jackknife
jackpot
jailbird
jawbone
jawbreaker
jaywalk
jellyfish
jerkwater
jerrybuild
jigsaw
jimsonweed
jitterbug
jobholder
johnnycake

K

keepsake
keyboard
keyhole
keynote
keystone
kickback
kickoff
kidnap
killdeer
killjoy

kindhearted
kingfisher
kinglet
kingpin
kinsfolk
kinship
kinsman
knapsack
kneecap
kneehole
knockout
knothole

L

lackluster
ladybug
ladyfinger
lambkin
lampblack
landfall
landholder
landlocked
landlord
landmark
landslide
landward
Lapland
lapwing
larkspur
laughingstock
lawgiver
lawmaker
lawsuit
layman
layoff
layout
layover
leapfrog
leasehold
leatherneck
leeward
leeway
leftovers
leghorn
letdown
letterhead
letterpress

levelheaded
lifeblood
lifeboat
lifeguard
lifelong
lifetime
lifework
liftoff
lightface
lightheaded
lighthearted
lighthouse
lightweight
likewise
limelight
limerick
limestone
lineman
linesman
lipstick
litterbug
liveryman
livestock
lockjaw
lockout
locksmith
locoweed
lodestar
lodestone
loggerhead
logjam
logrolling
loincloth
longhair
longhand
longshoreman
lookout
loophole
lopsided
lordship
loudmouth
lovebird
lovelorn
lovesick
lowboy
lowbrow
lowdown

lowland
lukewarm
lumberjack
lumberyard

M

madhouse
maidenhair
mailbox
mailman
mailroom
mainland
mainmast
mainsail
mainspring
mainstay
mainstream
makeshift
manhandle
manhole
manhood
manhunt
mankind
manlike
manpower
marketplace
marksman
markup
mastermind
masterpiece
masterwork
masthead
matchbook
matchlock
matchmaker
maybe
mayflower
meadow
mealtime
meantime
meanwhile
merrymaking
meshwork
middlebrow
middleman
middlemost
middleweight

midshipman
milestone
milkmaid
milkman
milksop
milkweed
millpond
millstone
millstream
minuteman
mockingbird
mockup
molehill
moleskin
monkeyshine
monkshood
moonlight
moonshine
moonstone
moonstruck
moreover
motherland
motorboat
motorcar
motorcycle
motorman
mouthpiece
muckrake
mudguard
mudslinger
muskmelon
muskrat

N

namesake
nearby
neckline
necktie
needlepoint
needlework
neighborhood
network
nevermore
newborn
newcomer
newsboy
newscast

newsletter
newspaper
newspaperman
newsprint
newsreel
newsstand
nightcap
nightclothes
nightclub
nightdress
nightfall
nightgown
nighthawk
nightmare
nightshade
nightshirt
nightstick
nighttime
nitwit
nobleman
nobody
noonday
noontide
noontime
northward
notebook
noteworthy
nothing
nowadays
nowhere
nowise
nursemaid
nurseryman
nutcracker
nuthatch
nutmeat
nutmeg
nutshell

O

oarlock
oarsman
oatmeal
offbeat
offend
offhand
officeholder

offset
offshoot
offshore
offside
offspring
oilcloth
oilskin
oncoming
oneself
ongoing
onionskin
onlooker
onrush
onset
onward
openhanded
openwork
otherwise
otherworldly
ourselves
outbid
outboard
outbound
outbreak
outbuilding
outburst
outcast
outclass
outcome
outcrop
outcry
outdated
outdistance
outdo
outdoor
outdoors
outermost
outface
outfield
outfit
outflank
outfox
outgo
outgoing
outgrow
outgrowth
outguess

outhouse	overanalyze	overexpansion	overrate
outlast	overanxious	overexpose	overreach
outlaw	overassertive	overextend	overreact
outlay	overbalance	overfeed	override
outline	overbear	overfill	overriding
outlive	overbearing	overflow	overripe
outlook	overbid	overfull	overrule
outlying	overblown	overgenerous	overrun
outmoded	overboard	overgraze	overseas
outnumber	overbold	overgrown	oversee
outpatient	overburden	overhand	oversell
outplay	overbuy	overhang	oversensitive
outpost	overcapacity	overhasty	oversexed
output	overcapitalize	overhaul	overshadow
outrage	overcast	overhead	overshoe
outreach	overcautious	overhear	overshoot
outrigger	overcharge	overheat	oversight
outright	overcoat	overindulge	oversimplify
outrun	overcome	overinflate	oversize
outsell	overcompensate	overinvest	oversleep
outset	overconfident	overkill	overspecialization
outshine	overcook	overland	overspecialize
outside	overcool	overlap	overspend
outsider	overcritical	overlarge	overspread
outsize	overcrowd	overlay	overstate
outskirts	overcurious	overleap	overstay
outsmart	overdelicate	overlie	overstep
outspoken	overdevelop	overload	overstock
outspread	overdo	overlong	overstretch
outstanding	overdose	overlook	overstuffed
outstation	overdraft	overlord	oversubscribe
outstay	overdramatize	overmaster	oversupply
outstretch	overdraw	overmatch	overtake
outstrip	overdress	overmodest	overtax
outward	overdrive	overmuch	overthrow
outwear	overdue	overnice	overtime
outweigh	overeager	overnight	overtire
outwit	overeat	overpass	overtone
outwork	overeducate	overpay	overtop
overabundance	overemotional	overplay	overturn
overabundant	overemphasis	overpopulate	overuse
overact	overemphasize	overpower	overvalue
overactive	overemphatic	overprice	overview
overage	overenthusiastic	overprint	overweening
overaggressive	overestimate	overproduce	overweigh
overall	overexcite	overprotect	overweight
overambitious	overexert	overqualified	overwhelm

overwork
overwrought
overzealous
oxbow
oxford

P

pacemaker
pacesetter
painkiller
painstaking
pancake
panhandle
paperback
paperhanger
paperweight
paperwork
parkway
passbook
passport
password
pasteboard
patchwork
pathfinder
pathway
pawnbroker
pawnshop
payload
paymaster
payoff
payroll
peacemaker
peacetime
peanut
peephole
peewee
penknife
penman
penmanship
pennyroyal
pennyweight
peppercorn
peppermint
pickax
pickpocket
pickup
pigeonhole

piggyback
pigheaded
pigpen
pigskin
pigsty
pigtail
pillbox
pillowcase
pilothouse
pincushion
pineapple
pinecone
pinfeather
pinhole
pinkeye
pinpoint
pinprick
pinstripe
pinup
pinwheel
pipeline
pitchfork
pitchman
pitfall
plainclothes
playbill
playboy
playgoer
playground
playmate
playpen
playroom
plaything
playwright
plowshare
plywood
pocketbook
pocketknife
pockmark
pointblank
polecat
polestar
policeman
poorhouse
popcorn
popeyed
popgun

popover
poppycock
portend
porterhouse
portfolio
porthole
potbelly
potboiler
potholder
pothole
pothook
potluck
potpie
powerboat
powerhouse
praiseworthy
pressman
prizefighter
proofread
puffball
pullover
purebred
pushcart
pushover
pussyfoot

Q

quarterback
quartermaster
quarterstaff
quicksand
quicksilver
quickstep

R

racecourse
racehorse
racetrack
ragtag
ragtime
ragweed
railroad
railway
rainbow
raincoat
rainfall

rainstorm
rainwater
ratline
rattlesnake
rattletrap
rawboned
rawhide
rearmost
rearrange
rearward
redcap
redcoat
reddish
redhead
redraft
redraw
redskin
redwood
rhinestone
ringleader
ringside
ringworm
ripcord
ripsaw
riverboat
riverside
roadbed
roadrunner
roadside
roadway
roebuck
roommate
rootstock
rosebud
rosemary
rosewood
roughhew
roughhouse
roughneck
roughshod
roundabout
roundhouse
roundup
rowboat
rubdown
rumrunner
runabout

runaway
runlet
runway

S

sackcloth
saddlebow
sadiron
safeguard
safekeeping
sagebrush
sailboat
sailfish
saltcellar
saltshaker
saltwater
sandalwood
sandbar
sandblast
sandbox
sandhog
sandman
sandpaper
sandpiper
sandstone
sandstorm
sapsucker
saucepan
sawbuck
sawdust
sawhorse
sawmill
scarecrow
scatterbrain
scholarship
schoolboy
schoolchild
schoolgirl
schoolhouse
schoolmaster
schoolmate
schoolmistress
schoolroom
schoolteacher
Scotchman
scrapbook
screenplay

screwball
screwdriver
seaboard
seacoast
seafarer
seafaring
seafood
seagoing
seaman
seamanship
seaplane
seaport
searchlight
seashell
seashore
seasickness
seaside
season
seaward
seaway
seaweed
seaworthy
secondhand
sendoff
setback
setup
shakedown
shakeup
shamefaced
sharecropper
shareholder
sharkskin
sharpshooter
sheepskin
shellfish
shipboard
shipbuilding
shipmate
shipshape
shipwreck
shipyard
shoehorn
shoelace
shoemaker
shoetree
shopkeeper
shoplifter

shopworn
shoreline
shortcake
shortchange
shortcoming
shorthand
shorthanded
shortsighted
shortstop
shotgun
showcase
showdown
showman
showoff
shuffleboard
shutdown
shuteye
shuttlecock
sickbay
sickbed
sideboard
sideburns
sidecar
sidekick
sideline
sidelong
sidereal
sidesaddle
sidestep
sidestroke
sideswipe
sidetrack
sidewalk
sideways
sightseeing
signboard
signpost
silkworm
silverfish
silversmith
silverware
singsong
sit-up
skullcap
skylark
skylight
skyline

skyrocket
skyscraper
skyward
skywriting
slapdash
slapstick
slaughterhouse
sledgehammer
sleepwalking
sleepyhead
slingshot
slipcover
slipknot
slipover
slipshod
smallpox
smokehouse
smokestack
smoothbore
snapdragon
snapshot
snowball
snowbound
snowdrift
snowdrop
snowfall
snowflake
snowplow
snowshoe
snowstorm
soapstone
softball
somebody
someday
somehow
someone
someplace
something
sometime
sometimes
someway
somewhat
somewhere
songbird
soundproof
soundtrack
sourpuss

southeast
southward
southwest
soybean
spacecraft
spaceman
spaceship
speakeasy
speedway
speedwell
spellbind
spellbinder
spellbound
spendthrift
spillway
sportsman
sportsmanship
sportswear
spotlight
springboard
Springfield
springtime
spyglass
stagecoach
staircase
stairway
stalemate
standby
standpipe
standstill
starboard
starfish
starlight
stateroom
stateside
statesman
steadfast
steamboat
steamroller
steamship
steeplechase
steeplejack
stepbrother
stepchild
stepdaughter
stepfather
stepladder

stepmother
stepparent
steppingstone
stepsister
stepson
stillbirth
stockbroker
stockholder
stockpile
stockyard
stopgap
stopwatch
storehouse
storekeeper
storeroom
stouthearted
stovepipe
stowaway
straightedge
straightforward
strawberry
streamlined
streetcar
streetwalker
strikeout
strongbox
stronghold
sugarplum
suitcase
summertime
sunburn
sundial
sundown
sundry
sunfish
sunflower
sunglasses
sunlight
sunlit
sunrise
sunset
sunshine
sunspot
sunstroke
sunup
superego
superhighway

superhuman
superman
supermarket
supernova
surfboard
swallowtail
sweepstakes
sweetbread
sweetbrier
sweetheart
sweetmeat
switchboard
swordfish
swordplay
swordsman

T

tablecloth
tableland
tablespoon
tableware
taillight
tailspin
takeoff
talebearer
tapeworm
taproom
taproot
taskmaster
tattletale
teammate
teardrop
teaspoon
teenager
telltale
tenderfoot
tenderhearted
tenderloin
tenpin
textbook
thanksgiving
themselves
thereabout
thereafter
thereat
thereby
therein

thereinafter
thereof
thereon
thereto
theretofore
thereunto
thereupon
therewith
thickset
thighbone
thistledown
thoroughbred
thoroughfare
thoroughgoing
threadbare
threescore
threesome
throughout
throughway
throwback
thumbnail
thumbscrew
thumbtack
thunderbolt
thunderclap
thundercloud
thunderhead
thunderstone
thunderstorm
thunderstruck
thundershower
tideland
tidewater
tightfisted
tightlipped
tightrope
tightwad
timberline
timekeeper
timepiece
timetable
timeworn
tinderbox
tinfoil
tinsmith
tintype
tiptoe

toadstool
toastmaster
toenail
tollgate
tomboy
tombstone
tomcat
toothpaste
toothpick
topcoat
topflight
topknot
topmost
topnotch
topsail
topsoil
tossup
touchdown
touchstone
townsman
townspeople
trademark
tradesman
trainman
trapshooting
treadmill
tribesman
troopship
troublemaker
truckload
truelove
trustworthy
tryout
tugboat
tumbleweed
turnabout
turncoat
turnout
turnover
turnpike
turnstile
turntable
turtledove
twosome
typeface
typesetter
typewrite

typewriter

U

underachieve
underarm
underbelly
underbid
underbred
underbrush
undercarriage
undercharge
underclassman
underclothes
undercoat
undercook
undercover
undercurrent
undercut
underdeveloped
underdog
underdone
undereducated
underemphasize
underemployed
underestimate
underexpose
underfeed
underfoot
undergarment
undergird
undergo
undergraduate
underground
undergrowth
underhand
underhanded
underlie
underline
underlying
undermine
undermost
underneath
undernourished
underpants
underpass
underpay
underpinning

underplay
underpowered
underprivileged
underproduction
underrate
underscore
undersea
undersecretary
undersell
undersexed
undershirt
undershorts
undershot
underside
undersigned
undersized
underskirt
understaffed
understand
understanding
understate
understood
understudy
undersupply
undersurface
undertake
undertaker
undertaking
undertone
undertow
undertrained
undervalue
underwater
underwear
underweight
underworld
underwrite
upbeat
upbraid
upbringing
upcoming
upcountry
update
updraft
upend
upgrade
uphill

uphold
upholster
upholstery
upkeep
upland
uplift
upon
uppercut
uppermost
upraise
upright
uprising
uproar
uproot
upset
upshot
upstage
upstairs
upstanding
upstart
upstate
upstream
upsurge
upswing
uptake
uptown
upturn
upward
uttermost

V

vainglory
viewpoint
vineyard
violoncello
volleyball
voltmeter
vouchsafe

W

waistcoat
waistline
walkout
walkup
wallboard
walleye

walleyed
wallflower
wallpaper
wardrobe
wardship
warehouse
warfare
warhead
warlike
warlock
warlord
warpath
warship
wartime
washboard
washcloth
washout
washroom
washstand
washtub
wasteland
watchdog
watchman
watchword
watercolor
waterfall
waterfowl
waterfront
watermark
watermelon
waterpower
waterproof
watershed
waterspout
watertight
waterway
waterworks
waveform
wavelength

waxwing
waxworks
wayside
weakfish
weatherboard
weathercock
weatherman
weatherproof
weekday
weekend
weightlifting
westward
wetback
whaleboat
whalebone
whatever
wheelbarrow
wheelbase
wheelchair
wheelwright
whereabouts
whereas
whereat
whereby
wherefore
wherefrom
wherein
whereof
whereon
whereto
whereupon
wherewith
whichever
whipcord
whipsaw
whirlpool
whirlwind
whiskbroom
whitecap

whitefish
whitewall
whitewash
wholehearted
wholesale
wholesome
whomever
widespread
wildcat
wildfire
wildfowl
wildlife
windburn
windfall
windflower
windlass
windmill
windowpane
windowsill
windpipe
windshield
windsock
windstorm
windswept
windward
wingspan
wingspread
wintergreen
wintertime
wiretap
wisecrack
wishbone
witchcraft
withdraw
withdrawn
withhold
within
without
withstand

wolfhound
womankind
wonderland
woodcarving
woodchuck
woodcraft
woodcut
woodcutter
woodland
woodpecker
woodsman
woodwork
woolgathering
workbench
workbook
workday
workhorse
workhouse
workman
workmanlike
workmanship
workout
workroom
workshop
worktable
worldwide
wormwood
worthwhile
wrongdoer

Y

yachtsman
yardarm
yardstick
yearbook
yourself

Exercise Answers

Chapter 1:

1-1: Exercise 1: Underline the *nouns* in each sentence.

1. <u>Emily</u> enjoys shopping.
2. <u>Mike</u> works at a <u>restaurant</u>.
3. <u>Sophia</u> likes to listen to <u>music</u>.
4. <u>Jim</u> is going to the <u>mall</u>.
5. <u>Jamie</u> has no <u>mail</u>.
6. <u>Shannon</u> lost the <u>wallet</u>.
7. <u>Michael</u> and <u>Tom</u> are <u>friends</u>.
8. <u>Seth</u> purchased a new <u>computer</u>.
9. <u>Chris</u> owns a <u>business</u>.
10. <u>Ann</u> wants to ride the <u>bike</u>.
11. My <u>cat</u> does not like <u>thunderstorms</u>.
12. The <u>store</u> was out of <u>eggs</u>.
13. Can <u>Luke</u> please have <u>pancakes</u> for <u>breakfast</u>?
14. <u>Mike</u> ordered <u>Jason's</u> birthday <u>present</u> three <u>days</u> ago.
15. How did <u>Mary</u> get <u>gum</u> stuck in <u>Ann's</u> <u>hair</u> again?
16. <u>Mom</u> found the <u>homework</u> on the floor.
17. Did <u>Michelle</u> send <u>Margaret</u> an <u>invitation</u> to the <u>party</u>?
18. Not even the <u>dog</u> would eat the <u>meatloaf</u>.
19. Did <u>Louis</u> hear the <u>teacher</u>?
20. <u>Sophia</u> took the <u>book</u> without asking.
21. <u>Carl</u> made <u>Jessica</u> a <u>sandwich</u>.

1-1: Exercise 2: Identify the *subject* and the *object* in each sentence.

1. Tim likes reading books.   subject = *Tim* / object = *books*
2. Tom is going to the store.   subject = *Tom* / object = *store*
3. Mary reads many magazines.   subject = *Mary* / object = *magazines*
4. Jack accidentally hit a car.   subject = *Jack* / object = *car*
5. Jim needs a laptop.   subject = *Jim* / object – *laptop*
6. Ben loves to go bowling.   subject = *Ben* / object = *bowling*
7. Chris must enter the movie theater.   subject = *Chris* / object = *theater*
8. Ann completed the work.   subject = *Ann* / object = *work*
9. Karen shopped at the mall.   subject = *Karen* / object = *mall*
10. The gardener dug into the ground.   subject = *gardener* / object = *ground*

1-2: Exercise 1: Underline the *vowel* in each sentence.

1. j <u>u</u> m p
2. s t <u>a</u> r t
3. w <u>o</u> m <u>a</u> n
4. p h <u>o</u> n <u>e</u>
5. l <u>i</u> g h t

1-2: Exercise 2: Underline the *consonant* in each sentence.

1. <u>p</u> <u>l</u> a <u>t</u> e
2. <u>p</u> a <u>p</u> e <u>r</u>
3. <u>d</u> o o <u>r</u>
4. <u>c</u> u <u>p</u>
5. <u>w</u> i <u>n</u> <u>d</u> o <u>w</u>

1-3: Exercise 1: Change each word to the *plural form*.

1. tax = taxes
2. lion = lions
3. map = maps
4. mix = mixes
5. pen = pens
6. box = boxes
7. ball = balls
8. chance = chances
9. paper = papers
10. note = notes

1-3: Exercise 2: Each word ends in –y. Change each word to the *plural* form.

1. mummy = mummies
2. family = families
3. key = keys
4. party = parties
5. berry = berries
6. army = armies
7. day = days
8. butterfly = butterflies
9. puppy = puppies
10. sky = skies
11. library = libraries
12. supply = supplies
13. bay = bays
14. valley = valleys
15. fly = flies

Chapter 2

2-1: Exercise 1: Imagine you are a world famous doctor, and your newest patient is coming to you because she has had the hiccups for three years and needs a cure. Using the *verbs* in the box, write suggestions for things she can do. Then, write a sentence telling us what you think is the best cure for the hiccups.

1. You should <u>drink</u> pickle juice.
2. <u>Eat</u> a spoonful of sugar.
3. Try to <u>breathe</u> into a paper bag.
4. <u>Imagine</u> a bunch of zebras running around.
5. <u>Hold</u> your breath for ten seconds.
6. <u>Say</u> a tongue twister.
7. Let someone <u>tickle</u> your feet.
8. <u>Hop</u> on one foot for thirty seconds.
9. <u>Smell</u> freshly popped popcorn.
10. Ask someone to <u>scare</u> you.

2-1: Exercise 2: Underline the *verb* in each sentence.

1. She *drives* slowly
2. My mom *is* a slow driver.
3. I *mow* my lawn frequently.
4. She *is* a quick walker.
5. She *walked* to the store quickly.
6. I *ran* to the school.
7. You must *enter* the movie theater quietly.
8. She *works* hard.
9. She *is* a poor student.
10. They *dug* deep into the ground.

2-2: Exercise 1: Write the correct *-ed* and *-ing* forms for the following words.

1. type – acting – acted
2. die – died – dying
3. erase – erased – erasing
4. fry – fried – frying
5. play – played – playing
6. cry – cried – crying
7. tie – tied – tying
8. study – studied – studying
9. hurry – hurried – hurrying
10. enjoy – enjoying – enjoyed

2-3: Exercise 1: Write the correct *-ed* and *-ing* forms for the following words.

1. act – acted – acting
2. look – looked – looking
3. bake – baked – baking
4. beg – begged – begging
5. continue – continued – continuing
6. cruise – cruised – cruising
7. edit – edited – editing
8. entertain – entertained – entertaining
9. equip – equipped – equipping
10. erase – erased – erasing
11. fan – fanned – fanning
12. heal – healed – healing
13. ignore – ignored – ignoring

2-3: Exercise 2: Write the correct *-ing* and *-ed* form for each *verb*.

1. robbing
2. stopped
3. beginning
4. dying
5. jumped
6. running
7. started
8. taking
9. required
10. completed
11. popping
12. chopping

2-4: Exercise 1: Give the correct *-ed* and *-ing* forms for the following words.

1. crush – crushed – crushing
2. drift – drifted – drifting
3. add – added – adding
4. wash – washed – washing
5. earn – earned – earning
6. stuff – stuffed – stuffing
7. melt – melted – melting
8. touch – touched – touching
9. scratch – scratched – scratching
10. invent – invented – inventing

2-5: Exercise 1: Practice the sentences below by answering *yes* to the following questions. Your answer should be similar to the answer given for the example.

1. Did you walk to school this morning?
   Answer: Yes, I walked to school this morning.
2. Question: Did you write that report?
   Answer: Yes, I wrote that report.
3. Question: Did you jog this morning?
   Answer: Yes, I jogged this morning.
4. Question: Did you wreck the car?
   Answer: Yes, I wrecked the car.
5. Question: Did he marry her?
   Answer: Yes, he married her.
6. Question: Did he accept the paper?
   Answer: Yes, he accepted the paper.
7. Question: Did they win the soccer game?
   Answer: Yes, they won the soccer game.
8. Question: Did you understand the material?
   Answer: Yes, I understood the material.
9. Question: Did you study for the math test?
   Answer: Yes, I studied for the math test.
10. Question: Did you hear me?
    Answer: Yes, I heard you.
11. Question: Did you know him?
    Answer: Yes, I knew him.

2-5: Exercise 2: Using the *irregular verb* list in the reference section, write the *simple past* and *past participle* forms of each word.

1. bite – bit – bitten
2. break – broke – broken
3. build – built – built
4. choose – chose – chosen
5. cut – cut – cut
6. find – found – found
7. forget – forgot – forgotten
8. freeze – froze – frozen
9. go – went – gone
10. know – knew – know

Chapter 3:

3-1 & 3-2: Exercise 1: Choose whether the sentence is *progressive* or *nonprogressive*.

1. nonprogressive
2. progressive
3. progressive
4. progressive
5. progressive
6. nonprogressive
7. nonprogressive
8. progressive
9. progressive
10. nonprogressive
11. nonprogressive
12. nonprogressive
13. progressive
14. progressive
15. progressive
16. nonprogressive
17. nonprogressive
18. nonprogressive
19. nonprogressive
20. progressive

3-3: Exercise 1: Answer each question using the *expression of place*. The location of the *subject* is in parenthesis.

1. Mom is working in (her/the) office.
2. Mike is relaxing at home.
3. Dad is driving to the store.
4. Jenny is sleeping in (her/the) bedroom.
5. I am traveling to California.
6. Tom is leaving for the airport.
7. The cat is hiding under the bed.
8. That great smell is coming from the kitchen.
9. The dog is playing underneath the table.
10. Jan is moving to New York.
11. Mike is going to the bookstore.

3-4: Exercise 1: Pretend your friend Michael has just bought a dog. Michael is stating problems that are wrong with his dog. Write Michael's complaints using the present progressive with *always*.

1. She's **always** barking loudly.
2. She's **constantly** breaking my things.

3. She's **forever** making me angry.
4. She's **constantly** stealing food.
5. She's **always** bringing dead birds in the house.
6. She's **constantly** chewing on my shoes.
7. She's **always** eating everything.
8. She's **always** fighting with other dogs.
9. She's **always** running away.
10. She's **constantly** biting people.
11. She's **always** scratching the furniture.

4-1: Exercise 1: Match the words from the box with the words in the exercise below. Choose the answer choices that make the most sense.

1. Lions growl.
2. Birds chirp.
3. Athletes compete.
4. Babies cry.
5. Plants grow.
6. Dogs bark.
7. Students learn.
8. Fish swim.
9. Musicians sing.
10. Artists paint.

4-2: Exercise 1: Pick the correct answer choice by writing either *transitive* or *intransitive*.

1. intransitive
2. intransitive
3. intransitive
4. transitive
5. intransitive
6. intransitive
7. transitive
8. transitive
9. intransitive
10. intransitive
11. transitive
12. transitive
13. intransitive
14. intransitive
15. transitive

Chapter 5

5-1: Exercise 1: Choose the correct verb by writing the corresponding letter in the blank.

1. She *is* running.
2. It *looks* like rain.
3. They *are* eating dinner.
4. My computer *is* black.
5. My teacher *is* nice.
6. You *need* to take a shower.
7. The bus *is* on time.
8. The taxi drivers *are* driving fast.
9. He *likes* to eat a lot.
10. She *is* late.

5-2: Exercise 1: Underline the correct *verb* for each sentence.

1. Josh and Tim (is / are) friends.
2. Mike and six other people (is / are) at school today.
3. John and four other people (don't / doesn't) want to take the bus.
4. The cat or dog (were / was) in the trash.
5. Mom and dad (were / was) yelling at the man.
6. She (don't / doesn't) want to go to the party.
7. He (don't / doesn't) want to go shopping.
8. It (don't / doesn't) look like it will rain.
9. Everyone (is / are) going to the park.
10. Somebody (is / are) in trouble.
11. Mike and I (don't / doesn't) want to go to Texas; we want to go to New York.
12. Jim and Sandy (is / are) getting married.
13. Nobody (is / are) going to the party at 8:00 p.m.
14. Each one (is / are) a different size.
15. My friends (is / are) traveling to Washington, D.C. for the July 4th parade.

5-2: Exercise 2: Determine whether the bold-printed verb in each sentence uses the correct verb form. If correct, write *correct*. If incorrect, rewrite the sentence with the correct form of the verb.

1. Carla **drove** to your house. Correct
2. Jason and Elizabeth **rides** their bikes every day. Incorrect-ride
3. Michelle **teach** kindergarten. Incorrect-teaches
4. Greg **live** in California. Incorrect-lives
5. Kari or Allison **has** the spare key. Correct
6. The only way to pass tests **are** to study. Incorrect-is
7. I **wants** to play football this season. Incorrect-want
8. Ohio and Pennsylvania **are** next to each other. Correct
9. The flowers you bought me **is** lovely. Incorrect-are
10. Every Thanksgiving, David and Maria **makes** pumpkin pie. Incorrect-make

11. Karen **needs** to borrow your car. <u>Correct</u>
12. She **make** coffee. <u>Incorrect-makes</u>

5-3: Exercise 1: Follow the rules of *subject/verb agreement* with *count/noncount nouns*, and choose the correct word for each sentence.

1. Seth and Beth (is/<u>are</u>) married.
2. Mike and Ben (<u>look</u> / looks) happy.
3. Mike and his dogs (is / <u>are</u>) taking a walk.
4. Mike or his friend (<u>is</u> / are) looking for the dog.
5. He (don't / <u>doesn't</u>) want to go to the store.
6. They (<u>don't</u> / doesn't) like traveling by car.
7. Someone (<u>is</u> / are) looking for the child's parents.
8. The weather (<u>is</u> / are) looking good.
9. The computers (is / <u>are</u>) broken.
10. The club (<u>is</u> / are) difficult to get into.

Chapter 6

6-1: Exercise 1: Fill in each blank with an *adjective* that makes sense.

1. When I asked Jessica for assistance, she was not very *helpful*.
2. I was so *embarrassed* when my dad started singing at the grocery store!
3. Matt is the *tallest* boy in the entire school.
4. It is *important* to read all of the instructions before beginning the assignment.
5. *Few* people can recite the entire Preamble of the Constitution.
6. Once the water is *boiling*, you can add the spaghetti.
7. Sheila is better than I am at playing the piano, but I think Mary is *best*.
8. Since I can't swim, I stay in the *shallow* end of the pool.
9. I am *angry* that I wasn't invited to the party.
10. Be *careful* what you wish for!

6-2: Exercise 1: Use an *adverb* from the box below to best complete each sentence. Each *adverb* is only used once.

1. It is <u>unlikely</u> that I will finish my homework before dinner.
2. <u>Yesterday</u> I told my aunt I'd babysit for her. Now I don't want to.
3. Brush your teeth twice <u>daily</u>.
4. This is where Dr. Martin Luther King Jr. <u>famously</u> delivered his "I Have a Dream" speech.
5. She <u>vaguely</u> remembers what the thief looked like.
6. It is hard to hear Karen because she speaks so <u>softly</u>.
7. After spinning around in circles, we <u>clumsily</u> fell down laughing.
8. When I <u>jokingly</u> told Amy that I didn't like her haircut, she cried.
9. When my sister left for college, we <u>tearfully</u> hugged and said goodbye.
10. After coming face to face with a snake, I backed away <u>slowly</u>, even though I wanted to run.

11. Carla <u>wisely</u> chose the correct answer and won a million dollars.
12. After doing <u>poorly</u> on the test, I asked Mrs. Peters for help after school.

6-2: Exercise 2: Write the correct *adverb* or *adjective* in each sentence.

1. She drives (slow, <u>slowly</u>).
2. My mom is a (<u>slow</u>, slowly) driver.
3. I mow my lawn (frequent, <u>frequently</u>).
4. She is a (<u>quick</u>, quickly) walker.
5. She walked to the store (quick, <u>quickly</u>).
6. I am (rare, <u>rarely</u>) on that side of town.
7. You must enter the movie theater (quiet, <u>quietly</u>).
8. She does her work (poor, <u>poorly</u>).
9. She is a (<u>poor</u>, poorly) student.
10. They dug (<u>deep</u>, deeply) into the ground.
11. She drew a (<u>beautiful</u>, beautifully) portrait.
    She drew the portrait (beautiful, <u>beautifully</u>).

6-3: Exercise 1: Choose the correct adjective clause for each sentence.

1. Mike has a dog <u>that</u> chews up many things. (whose / when / that)
2. I know a friend <u>whose</u> mother is the president of a company. (whose / that / when)
3. I know a place <u>where</u> the chicken is outstanding. (when / where / that)
4. Dr. Linda, <u>whom</u> my friend loves, is not accepting patients. (that / when / whom)
5. My cat, <u>who</u> is the best cat in the world, loves mice. (when / whose / who)
6. The computer <u>that</u> I wanted to buy is too expensive. (that / where / when)
7. The police have not caught the person <u>who</u> hit my car yesterday. (when / whose / who)
8. The book <u>that</u> I borrowed from Linda has been stolen. (when / where / that)
9. That time <u>when</u> I lost my dog was very sad for me. (when / where / that)
10. The man <u>whose</u> house I am looking to purchase is willing to lower the price. (whose / that / when)

Chapter 7

7-1: Exercise 1: Complete each *contraction*.

1. could + not = <u>couldn't</u>
2. <u>she</u> + would = she'd
3. <u>I</u> + am = I'm
4. <u>had</u> + not = hadn't
5. might + have = <u>might've</u>
6. it + <u>will</u> = It'll
7. will + not = <u>won't</u>
8. <u>we</u> + are = we're
9. <u>you</u> + will = you'll
10. what + have = <u>what've</u>

11. Do + <u>not</u> = don't

7-1: Exercise 2: Change each word phrase into a *contraction*.

1. <u>It's</u> for sale.
2. <u>I'm</u> a student.
3. The car <u>isn't</u> for sale.
4. <u>I'll</u> go to the store.
5. <u>It's</u> been great.
6. <u>They've</u> gone to the store.
7. <u>You're</u> out of pretzels.
8. <u>We're</u> out of time.
9. <u>We'll</u> be back at 5:00pm.
10. <u>She'd</u> go to the store if she had a car.

7-2: Exercise 1: Choose the correct *article* for each sentence.

1. Question: Do you have <u>the</u> homework I assigned yesterday?
   Answer: Yes, I do.
2. Question: Do you have <u>a</u> pencil?
   Answer: Yes, I do.
3. Question: Do you have <u>an</u> idea?
   Answer: Yes, I absolutely do.
4. Question: Do you have <u>a</u> soda?
   Answer: Yes, we do.
5. Question: Do you have <u>a</u> dog?
   Answer: Yes, I do.
6. Question: Does she work in <u>an</u> office?
   Answer: Yes, she does.
7. Question: Is he <u>an</u> orphan?
   Answer: No, he isn't.
8. Question: Do you have <u>a</u> pencil?
   Answer: No, I don't have pencil.
9. Question: Do you have <u>the</u> book you borrowed?
   Answer: Yes, I have the book.
10. Question: Can I use <u>the</u> computer?
    Answer: Yes, you can use the computer.
11. Question: Can I have <u>the</u> money you owe me?
    Answer: Yes, you can.

Chapter 8

8-1 through 8-5: Exercise 1: Use either *simple present* or *present progressive* to change the words in parenthesis to the correct form.

1. Mike cannot come outside because he *is cleaning* his room.
2. Mike *cleans* his room every day.
3. Ashley is *sleeping* right now. Can you come back later?
4. It *rains* a lot in Seattle.
5. Seth *runs* every day after school.
6. It *snows* in Ohio.
7. I *watch* TV every day after school.
8. She *runs* errands each day between 2:00pm and 4:00pm.
9. It is *hailing* right now in Florida.
10. The volcano has lava *flowing* out of the top.
11. I *bike* to work on Fridays.

8-1 through 8-5: Exercise 2: Use *past perfect* to change the words in parenthesis to the correct form.

1. I *studied* the information before I took my driving test.
2. I *cleaned* my room three days ago.
3. She *slept* for two hours before I came in and woke her up.
4. He *looked* at the material before he took the test.
5. My boss *asked* me to work yesterday, so I cannot go to the mall today.

8-1 through 8-5: Exercise 3: Use future *progressive* to change the words in parenthesis to the correct form.

1. I *will work* today, so come by and visit me.
2. I *will call* you after school.
3. I *will discuss* this with your father after school.
4. She *will study* all afternoon.
5. She *will talk* to the professor after class.

Chapter 9

9-1: Exercise 1: Complete the sentence with the correct *gerund* form.

1. *Running* is my favorite exercise.
2. I love *reading*.
3. *Reading* is a good way to learn English.
4. A good outdoor activity is *biking*.
5. *Speaking* is my favorite part about learning.
6. Tom's favorite activity is *hiking*.
7. Bird *watching* is my favorite activity.

8. *Driving* is difficult for me.
9. *Listening* to my mother speak is difficult.
10. *Typing* is the best way to write your school papers.

9-2: Exercise 1: Underline the *gerund-phrase* combination in each sentence.

1. The author liked writing the book.
2. The musician enjoyed playing the instrument.
3. The athlete began running at noon.
4. The girl continued talking to her friend.
5. The student kept typing on her computer.
6. The mom started yelling at her child.
7. The teacher allowed talking in his class.
8. The artist stopped painting after he sold his artwork.
9. They liked going the store.
10. My mom keeps cleaning my room.
11. They enjoy traveling to the beach.
12. Mike likes listening to the professor.
13. Mary suggested running the marathon.
14. Ann likes participating in class.
15. The teacher likes giving us homework.

9-3: Exercise 1: Write the gerund that makes the most sense.

1. The teacher wanted us learning.
2. The coach needed her practicing.
3. The musician loved Gloria's singing.
4. My best friend really appreciated me listening to her problems.
5. The furniture buyer worried about the carpenter crafting the wrong chair.
6. I needed the student studying.
7. I took the car to the mechanic and said, "I need the car working."
8. The doctor needed the patient resting.
9. The priest wanted them praying.
10. We needed the architect designing.

9-4: Exercise 1: Write the correct *go + gerund* form for each sentence.

1. I like to go fishing.
2. I go walking everyday
3. Tom goes running in the afternoons.
4. Mary is going exercise.
5. We are going swimming.
6. Ann is going hiking.
7. The students are going studying.
8. The mother goes jogging every day after work.
9. Tom goes smoking every afternoon.

10. Lisa is <u>going shopping</u>.

Chapter 10

10-1: Exercise 1: Complete the sentence with the correct *infinitive* or *gerund* form.

1. The artist only likes <u>to paint</u>.
2. Tom loves the outdoors and his favorite activity is <u>to hike</u>.
3. When I go to class, my teacher always tells me <u>to listen</u>.
4. The architect loves <u>to design</u>.
5. The baseball player wants <u>to train</u>.
6. The doctor has chosen <u>to treat</u> his patient.
7. The author likes <u>to write</u> in the evening.
8. The singer refuses <u>to perform</u> for small crowds.
9. I do not understand why my computer refuses <u>to print</u>.
10. I cannot get my MP3 <u>to play</u>.

10-2: Exercise 1: Choose the correct *verb* from the box above. Then change the *verb* to an *infinitive* to complete the sentence.

1. My dad <u>needs</u> to ask for directions.
2. Why did you <u>fail</u> to tell me that I needed to bring my swimsuit?
3. I <u>need</u> to start studying as soon as the movie is over.
4. I don't <u>care</u> to hold your pet snake.
5. I <u>agreed</u> to make three dozen cookies for the party.
6. Don't <u>forget</u> to brush your teeth!
7. I <u>happen</u> to know the owner of the restaurant.
8. Let's <u>attempt</u> to answer your questions.
9. I can't <u>begin</u> to understand what you are going through.
10. Maria can't <u>afford</u> to fail another Biology test.

10-3: Exercise 1: Complete each sentence with the correct *infinitive* form.

1. The coach wanted his athletes <u>to practice</u>.
2. My teacher wanted me <u>to learn</u>.
3. The banker wanted me <u>to deposit</u>, not withdrawal.
4. The gardener wanted me <u>to dig</u>.
5. The music teacher wanted me <u>to sing</u>.

10-4: Exercise 1: You are Christopher Columbus and your crew is ready to turn the ships around and head back home. The sentences below are things you may say to your crew to keep them motivated. Underline the *noun* and *infinitive* phrases in each sentence below.

1. Every <u>attempt to</u> turn the ship around has failed.
2. Don't you understand that I have a <u>need to</u> see the rest of the world?
3. The king and queen have granted <u>permission to</u> explore.
4. It is my <u>wish to</u> see land.

5. There is a <u>way to</u> get around the world that we haven't seen yet!
6. This is a <u>reminder to</u> always dream!
7. I have a <u>goal to</u> explore every inch of this world.
8. I have a <u>plan to</u> find gold and other riches.
9. It is my <u>decision to</u> keep sailing. We will reach land soon!
10. If there is any <u>refusal to</u> keep sailing, we will throw you overboard!

10-5: Exercise 1: Underline the *be+adjective+infinitive* combinations in the paragraph below. There are ten.

It's going to <u>be sad to</u> move away from my hometown, but my mom said I should realize how great it is to go to a new city. "Other kids would <u>be fortunate to</u> have a new city with new friends!" is what she keeps telling me. You'd <u>be amazed to</u> see how many friends I already have here, is what I keep telling her. I'll <u>be certain to</u> keep in touch with everyone. I guess I should <u>be grateful to</u> at least go to a city that is on the beach. My older sister is really excited. She thinks our hometown is so boring, but I think she should <u>be proud to</u> live here! She doesn't think I should <u>be scared to</u> move, but I love my house, and I love my friends! I'll <u>be sorry to</u> leave everything behind! I guess I have to <u>be willing to</u> try something new. She said I will <u>be relieved to</u> know that my new school is in walking distance to our new house. I guess that makes me feel a little better.

10-6: Exercise 1: Rewrite each sentence placing the word *too* in the correct place. Then, complete the sentence with the correct *infinitive*.

1. The car is too old to drive.
2. The light is too dim to see.
3. The music is too loud to study.
4. The computer is too expensive to purchase.
5. The box is too heavy to purchase.
6. It is too hot to run.
7. The bridge is too icy to cross.
8. The library is too quite to talk.
9. The pool is too shallow to dive.
10. They are too excited to sleep.
11. The company is too big to fail.

10-6: Exercise 2: The word *too* has been taken out of all of the sentences. Rewrite each sentence placing the word *too* in the correct place in each sentence. Then, finish each sentence using one of the phrases from the box above.

1. The music is too loud to have a conversation.
2. It's too cold outside to not wear a jacket.
3. The water is too cold to go swimming.
4. She is too slow to run a race.
5. The book is too long to read in one day.
6. David is too full to eat another bite.
7. Mike is too poor to pay his bills.
8. Jessica is too careful to make mistakes.

9. The sky is too dark to wear sunglasses.
10. Arthur is too nervous to speak in public.
11. The computer is too broken to type my paper.

10-7: Exercise 1: The word *enough* has been taken out of all of the sentences. Rewrite each sentence placing the word *enough* in the correct place in each sentence.

1. She doesn't have *enough* money to go to the movies.
2. Tom has *enough* money to buy his bike.
3. You must drink *enough* to hydrate yourself.
4. They must practice *enough* English to speak well.
5. She did not run fast *enough* to win the marathon race.
6. Tom did not swim quick *enough* to win the meet.
7. The joke was not funny *enough* to laugh.
8. The water was not warm *enough* to take a shower.
9. They did not read *enough* to take the test.
10. She did not talk *enough* to receive the job.

Chapter 11

11-1: Exercise 1: Identify the *antecedent* and the *pronoun* in each sentence.

1. antecedent: game / pronoun: It
2. antecedent: gorillas / pronoun: they
3. antecedent: mother / pronoun: she
4. antecedent: remote / pronoun: it
5. antecedent: potato chips / pronoun: they
6. antecedent: Statue of Liberty / pronoun: it
7. antecedent: young man / pronoun: he
8. antecedent: light bulb / pronoun: it
9. antecedent: brothers / pronoun: they
10. antecedent: grandfather / pronoun: he

11-2: Exercise 1: Rewrite the following sentences using *personal pronouns* as the *subject*.

1. John was waiting for the rain to stop.
   He was waiting for the rain to stop.
2. Elizabeth has never seen the movie.
   She has never seen the movie.
3. Lewis and Clark explored America.
   They explored America.
4. Jason made everyone dinner.
   He made everyone dinner.
5. The remote was under a sofa cushion.
   It was under a sofa cushion.
6. My dentist told me that I didn't need braces. I didn't believe him.

He told me that I didn't need braces. I didn't believe him.

11-2: Exercise 2: In the sentences below, fill in the blank with the correct *subject pronouns*.

1. Kelly wants to go shopping. <u>She</u> needs new shoes.
2. David likes riding his bike around town. <u>He</u> says it's the best form of exercise.
3. Jessica and I don't agree on everything, but <u>we</u> do agree on what movie to see.
4. Mrs. Richards graded our tests. <u>She</u> said we all passed.
5. Greg and Linda missed recess today. <u>They</u> had to make up a test.
6. If Missy doesn't tell us what kind of ice cream to buy, <u>she</u> will just have to settle for vanilla.
7. The cat is happily sleeping. <u>It</u> only wakes up for meals.
8. The play takes place in Pittsburgh. <u>It</u> is based on a true story.
9. Debbie and Heather are working hard. <u>They</u> are always competing with each other.
10. The coach said I that need to practice more. <u>He/She</u> thinks I could be a lot faster.
11. The musicians are trying to sell their CD. <u>They</u> think it will make them rich!

11-3: Exercise 1: Underline the correct *pronoun* that makes the sentence grammatically correct.

1. (<u>They</u> / She) are going to the store.
2. (They / <u>She</u>) loves to walk in the park.
3. (<u>You</u> / She) have to study for the test tomorrow.
4. (<u>They</u> / He) live in New York City.
5. (<u>It</u> / They) grows very fast.
6. Mike read to (he /<u>him</u>).
7. Louis runs with (she / <u>her</u>).
8. I need to talk to (<u>you</u> / she).
9. The teacher likes to talk to (<u>us</u> / he).
10. I returned (<u>it</u> / us) to the library.

11-3: Exercise 2: Fill in the blank with the correct *object pronoun*.

1. I want to go to a movie tomorrow. You should come with <u>me</u>!
2. You have to stay after school. The teacher wants to talk to <u>you</u>.
3. I forgot my pencil. Lend one to <u>me</u>.
4. Jeffrey lost his retainer. His mom is going to be really mad at <u>him</u>.
5. I built a huge snowman. I used mom's old coat to keep <u>it</u> warm.
6. She forgot her lunch. I gave half of my sandwich to <u>her</u>.
7. The cat followed Mary home. She brought <u>it</u> inside.
8. You guys are making too much noise! The teacher is going to tell <u>you</u> to stop.
9. They want to build a tree house. It would keep <u>them</u> busy during the summer.
10. Why is everyone whispering? What secret are you keeping from <u>me</u>?

11-3: Exercise 3: Using both *object* and *subject pronouns*, fill in the blank using either *I* or *me*.

1. My mom and <u>I</u> went shopping.
2. Listen to <u>me</u>.

3. It's time for <u>me</u> to go home.
4. <u>I</u> have to clean my room before my parents get home.
5. The reward was split between my brother and <u>me</u>.
6. <u>I</u> tried my hardest but I still got a bad grade on my test.

Chapter 12

12-1 and 12-2: Exercise 1: Fill in the correct *intensive* or *reflexive noun*.

1. You *yourself* must clean your room.
2. They *themselves* are responsible for the mess.
3. I *myself* am responsible for the car accident.
4. We *ourselves* will have to fix our home.
5. She talks to *herself* when she is alone.
6. Mike and I talk to *ourselves* quietly.
7. Have you looked at *yourself* in the mirror?
8. He must tell *himself* he can win the race.
9. I looked at *myself* in the reflection* of the car.
10. The dog saw *itself* in the mirror and ran away.

12-3: Exercise 1: Choose the correct *demonstrative pronoun*. Use the word *this, that, these* or *those* to complete the sentence.

1. If you look up the hill, *that* is my house.
2. *These* keys you are touching are important.
3. *Those* restaurants in the other city are expensive.
4. *This* restaurant we are in looks nice.
5. *That* book bag in the other room is mine.
6. *This* award you are touching belongs to my grandfather. Be careful!
7. *These* drinks we are drinking are disgusting.
8. Do not drink *those* drinks on the other side of the room. They are not good.
9. *This* map we are next to is old.
10. *Those* trees in Oregon are huge.

12-4: Exercise 1: Using the *indefinite pronouns* in the box below, complete the sentences.

1. Does <u>anyone</u> know what time it is?
2. There is <u>nothing</u> to be afraid of.
3. <u>Everybody</u> gets sad once in a while.
4. I would do <u>anything</u> to get out of washing the dishes!
5. <u>No one</u> wanted dessert because we <u>all</u> ate too much.
6. Because <u>everyone</u> failed the spelling test, we have to review as a class.
7. <u>Both</u> Elizabeth and Patricia know how to play the piano.
8. <u>Few</u> people can name all the state capitals.
9. If you have <u>something</u> to say, say it!
10. <u>Someone</u> should teach her a lesson.

12-4: Exercise 2: Underline the *indefinite pronoun* for each sentence.

1. Yes, give me (<u>all</u> / everything) of it.
2. (<u>Everyone.</u> / All.)
3. Yes, I like (everybody / <u>both</u>) of them.
4. I want (nobody / <u>everything</u>).
5. Give me a (<u>few</u> / everybody) of them.
6. No, it's (<u>no one</u> / everyone). It's just the wind.
7. (<u>Neither</u> / Everyone) of them.
8. Ask (<u>another</u> / everybody) person.
9. There are too (everyone / <u>many</u>) people at the store.
10. (<u>None</u> / Any) of my college applications came in the mail today.

12-5: Exercise 1: Choose the correct *interrogative pronoun*.

1. <u>Who</u> went to the store?
2. <u>What</u> book did she buy?
3. <u>Whom</u> did you ask?
4. <u>Whose</u> book is this?
5. <u>Whoever</u> stole my book, please give it back.
6. <u>Whatever</u> you want, I will do it.
7. <u>Whoever</u> wants to go to the store, come with me now?
8. <u>Whichever</u> product you want to choose is ok with me.
9. <u>Which</u> book are you reading?
10. <u>What</u> is your favorite color?
11. <u>What</u> do you want to eat for dinner?
12. <u>Who</u> is making all of that noise?
13. <u>Who</u> needs help with homework?
14. <u>Which</u> of these do you like more?
15. <u>Which</u> way do we turn?
16. The bouquet of flowers is for <u>whom</u>?
17. To <u>whom</u> should I address the envelope?
18. <u>Whose</u> shoes are in the middle of the floor?
19. <u>Whose</u> jacket is missing a button?

12-6: Exercise 1: Using the *pronoun* definition list provided above chose the correct *relative pronoun*.

1. The person <u>who</u> is driving must remember to fill the car with gas.
2. The person <u>that</u> I saw yesterday was tall with dark hair.
3. The direction <u>that</u> I want to go is <u>whichever</u> direction you want to go.
4. The person <u>whose</u> shoes are off must put them on.
5. The man <u>whom</u> he admires is his father.

12-6: Exercise 2: Underline the *relative pronoun* in each sentence.

1. The book <u>that</u> you told me to read is really funny!
2. This is a warning <u>that</u> is difficult to ignore.
3. I'm not sure <u>whose</u> story is the scariest.
4. Because I won first prize in the contest, I can choose <u>whichever</u> prize I want.
5. I rented the apartment <u>that</u> is on Liberty Avenue.
6. I can't believe I ran into the man <u>who</u> found my missing purse.
7. Is there a place <u>where</u> I can buy a new hat?
8. I don't know <u>what</u> happened.
9. This is the man <u>whose</u> wife was my teacher.
10. Bring me the book <u>that</u> is on the table.

Chapter 13

13-1: Exercise 1: Choose the correct *possessive pronoun* for each sentence. Look at the noun(s) in bold to help you choose your answer.

11. That book belongs to *me*, so that book is (<u>mine</u> / theirs).
12. That pencil belongs to *him*, so that book is (hers / <u>his</u>).
13. Those shoes belong to *us*, so those shoes are (his / <u>ours</u>).
14. These keys belong to *them*, so these keys are (<u>theirs</u> / his).
15. The radio belongs to *her*, so the radio is (<u>hers</u> / theirs).
16. This book bag belongs to *Mike*, so this book bag is (<u>his</u> / hers).
17. The notepads belong to the *church*; these notepads are (<u>theirs</u> / his).
18. The cell phone belongs to *Susan*, so the cell phone is (<u>hers</u> / theirs).
19. The statue belongs to the *city*, so the statue is (hers / <u>theirs</u>).
20. The books belong to *him and me*, so the book is (<u>ours</u> / his).

13-1: Exercise 2: Underline the *possessive pronoun* in the sentence.

1. The paper is <u>yours</u>.
2. Those books are <u>theirs</u>, but you can borrow them.
3. That watch is <u>hers</u>.
4. These clothes are <u>ours</u>, but we're giving them away.
5. The iPod is <u>mine</u>.

13-1: Exercise 3: Underline the *possessive adjectives* in the sentence.

1. <u>Your</u> book is on the table.
2. <u>My</u> pencil is dull. (dull: not sharp)
3. <u>Your</u> TV is on.
4. If you eat that candy, <u>your</u> teeth will rot. (rot = be bad)
5. <u>My</u> iPod is broken.

14-1: Exercise 1: Re-write the following questions to make a *negative question*.

1. Did you study for the test?
   Did you not study for the test?
   Didn't you study for the test?
2. Can you ask her for help?
   Can't you ask for help?
   Can you not ask for help?
3. Will you join us for dinner?
   Won't you join us for dinner?
   Will you not join us for dinner?
4. Do you want more time?
   Don't you want more time?
   Do you not want more time?
5. Could you wait ten more minutes?
   Couldn't you wait ten more minutes?
   Could you not wait ten more minutes?
6. Are they serving pizza today in the cafeteria?
   Aren't they serving pizza today in the cafeteria?
   Are they not serving pizza today in the cafeteria?
7. Do you like roller coasters?
   Don't you like roller coasters?
   Do you not like roller coasters?

14-1: Exercise 2: Answer the following *negative questions* using a complete sentence.

1. No, I will not miss seeing you every day.
2. Yes, I am tired.
3. Yes, he has two cats.
4. Yes, she is from Canada.
5. No, I am not the oldest of five children.
6. No, I haven't eaten cereal every day for the past year.

14-3: Exercise 1: Write the correct *question word* for each question.

1. Question: Who is the woman?
2. Question: What time is it?
3. Question: When are you leaving?
4. Question: Where is my book?
5. Question: Why are you happy?
6. Question: How do you draw?
7. Question: Whose notebook is this?

14-3: Exercise 2: You have been given a once-in-a-lifetime chance to travel back in time and interview Ben Franklin. Read the paragraph below, and answer the questions.

1. I am going to interview Ben Franklin.
2. The interview will take place in Philadelphia.
3. I want to interview Ben Franklin because he is really interesting.
4. I will set the time machine to July 1776.
5. I will just sit him down and tell him the truth.
6. The paper will be ready on January 17.
7. I chose Ben Franklin because his birthday is the same date as the paper's due date.
8. I hope I get an A on my paper.
9. I will try to bring Ben Franklin back with me in my time machine.
10. Ben Franklin helped to draft and sign the Declaration of Independence.

Chapter 15

15-1 through 15-3: Exercise 1: Write the correct *preposition*.

1. to
2. at
3. in
4. on
5. at
6. on
7. at
8. on
9. on/in
10. in (for is possible, meaning that you stayed in Florida for the whole month)

15-1 through 15-3: Exercise 2: Write the correct *preposition*.

1. in (for could be used, meaning that you will be away for a period of time, in this case, three days)
2. in
3. in
4. on
5. to
6. on
7. to/from/to
8. on
9. in
10. on/during/for

15-1 through 15-3: Exercise 3: Write the correct *preposition.*

1. down
2. to
3. across/over
4. along/to/by
5. down
6. off
7. around
8. into/in
9. on
10. through

15-4: Exercise 1: Choose an *adjective* from column A or a preposition from column B to complete the sentences below.

1. I am *afraid of making* a mistake.
2. Kelly is *happy about winning* first place.
3. Tina is *responsible for collecting* money for our class trip.
4. Everyone is *worried about failing* the test.
5. I am *guilty of eating* too much at Thanksgiving.
6. We are all *disappointed in placing* last.
7. I am *scared of getting* lost in a new town.
8. Tony is *bored with listening* to his sister play piano.
9. We are all *responsible for making* our own lunches.
10. Kelly will be *remembered for singing* off-key in the musical. It was awful!

15-5: Exercise 1: Using the word box above, complete the sentences with the correct <u>verb</u> and <u>preposition</u> combination.

Dear Uncle David and Aunt Lucy,

Let me <u>begin by</u> telling you how great it was to see you at my birthday party. It was great to see you both, and Uncle David, you looked great in your new suit and tie. That being said, let me <u>apologize for</u> spilling my red punch all over your clothes. I also am sorry that you were hit with so many paintball pellets. I think we were all just trying to <u>concentrate on</u> shooting anyone who came past us, and when you walked through the playing field, we assumed it was to be part of the fun, not because you were trying to get to you car to change your clothes. You should have been <u>warned against</u> getting so dressed up for an eleven-year-old's party, especially when its theme is "paintball."

<u>Thanks for</u> giving me a check for my birthday. For the last year, I have <u>dreamt about</u> buying a television for my bedroom, and initially, any money I had I would <u>use for</u> making that happen. It would be an <u>escape from</u> living in a house full of eight older sisters and not having to <u>worry about</u>

fighting over the remote every time I want to watch my favorite TV show. (I never get to choose what to watch.)

After hearing about how much money your suit cost, my mom is insisting that I pay for you to buy a new suit. Even though I don't <u>agree with</u> making a kid <u>pay for</u> buying a grown-up a new suit (again, the theme was paintball), I will. That being said, I will <u>rely on</u> seeing photos of the new suit to know this is what the money was used for.

Sincerely,
Joseph

15-6: Exercise 1: Make the underlined phrase into a *gerund*.

1. process of <u>sewing</u>
2. story about <u>building</u>
3. love of <u>reading</u>
4. fear of <u>flying</u>
5. delay in <u>playing</u>
6. reputation for <u>singing</u>
7. memory of <u>swimming</u>

15-6: Exercise 2: Use the phrases above to complete the sentences.

1. I can't figure out the <u>process of sewing</u>, so my shirt is missing three buttons.
2. My mom has a <u>fear of flying</u>. We drive everywhere for vacation.
3. She has a <u>love of watching</u> movies in 3D.
4. I just read a <u>story about building</u> skyscrapers.
5. She has a <u>reputation for singing</u> incredibly off-key.
6. The rain has caused a <u>delay in playing</u> the championship game.

15-7: Exercise 1: Use the *subordinate clauses* below to complete the sentences. *Note: Some sentences will use more than one.*

1. Don't brush your teeth <u>until after</u> you've finished your orange juice.
2. <u>Although</u> the cake looked delicious, it tasted terrible.
3. I have to make sure my sister doesn't miss the bus <u>because</u> if she is late one more time, she will get a detention.
4. <u>If</u> you are going to the store, will you please buy milk?
5. I will wait for you after school <u>even though</u> I don't want to miss my favorite TV show.

15-7: Exercise 2: Underline the *subordinate clauses* in each sentence.

1. <u>After</u> the play ended, the audience applauded.
2. I don't want to go to the party <u>unless</u> Shelly is invited as well.
3. You are eating peas tonight <u>whether</u> you want to or not.
4. <u>Even though</u> I set three alarms this morning, I still managed to be late for my interview.
5. <u>Once</u> you start eating potato chips, it's hard to stop.

15-8: Exercise 1: Underline the *verb + preposition* in each sentence below.

1. I am <u>asking for</u> help.
2. We have <u>agreed on</u> a price for the baseball card.
3. Jessica will <u>apologize for</u> yelling at you.
4. We can't <u>argue about</u> everything!
5. My mom <u>decided to</u> care for my grandfather after he had a stroke.
6. I <u>belong to</u> three different teams.
7. I don't <u>care about</u> the weather! We play inside!
8. Do you still <u>communicate with</u> your old neighbor?
9. I will <u>apply for</u> an after-school job.
10. I still <u>believe in</u> the tooth fairy.

Chapter 16

16-1: Exercise 1: Is each noun a *common* or *proper noun*? Underline the correct answer.

1. Eiffel Tower (<u>common</u> / proper)
2. The White House (common / <u>proper</u>)
3. clock (<u>common</u> / proper)
4. New York Times (common / <u>proper</u>)
5. Mike (common / <u>proper</u>)
6. English (common / <u>proper</u>)
7. Los Angeles, CA (common / <u>proper</u>)
8. bank (<u>common</u> / proper)
9. United States (common / <u>proper</u>)
10. Tuesday (common / <u>proper</u>)

16-2: Exercise 1: You must change the *regular noun* to an *irregular noun*.

1. foot = <u>feet</u>
2. man = <u>men</u>
3. child = <u>children</u>
4. woman = <u>women</u>
5. mouse = <u>mice</u>
6. fish = <u>fish</u>
7. sheep = <u>sheep</u>
8. tooth = <u>teeth</u>
9. curriculum = <u>curricula</u>
10. deer = <u>deer</u>
11. louse = <u>lice</u>

16-3: Exercise 1: Complete the *compound noun* using the word box above.

1. foot<u>ball</u>
2. day<u>time</u>

3. grasshopper
4. grandmother
5. daydream
6. dogfight
7. quarterback
8. sailboat
9. teaspoon
10. turnpike

Chapter 17

17-1: Exercise 1: Complete the sentences with the correct form of the *possessive*

1. (Seth) Mike had gone to Seth's house because
2. Mike's car had broken down and he needed to call a tow truck.
3. (Seth) Seth's phone wasn't working so Seth had gone to Mike's next-door-neighbor – Louis.
4. (Louis) Louis' phone was working and Mike called a tow truck.
   While Mike was waiting for the tow truck, there were many boys outside playing.
5. (boy) The boy's ball had been stuck in tree.
6. (Charles) A boy walked over to Mike and said "Charles' ball was in a tree,
7. (Mike) and with Mike's help, the boys could get the ball out of the tree."
8. (tree) Mike went to the tree and climbed up the tree's thick branches.
   Mike got the ball and after he climbed down the tree, the boy said, "thank you."
9. (Mike) At that moment, Mike's tow truck came and Mike left with the tow truck repairperson.

17-2: Exercise 1: Look at the noun below. If it is a *count noun*, write *count* on the line. If it is a *noncount noun*, write *noncount*.

1. glass noncount
2. flour noncount
3. flower count
4. chalkboard count
5. chalk noncount
6. soccer noncount
7. soccer ball count
8. poetry noncount
9. homework noncount
10. assignment count

17-2: Exercise 2: Is the highlighted word a *noncount* or a *count noun*?

1. Can I have some *coffee*? noncount noun
2. I love your *furniture*. noncount noun
3. Do you have a *pencil*? count noun

4. I don't have any *money*. <u>noncount noun</u>
5. Drink lots of *water*. <u>noncount noun</u>
6. I love listening to *CD's*. <u>count noun</u>
7. There is too much *oil* on my pizza. <u>noncount noun</u>
8. Eat an **apple** instead of a *cookie*. <u>count noun</u>
9. Do you have a *pair of scissors*? <u>count noun</u>
10. They dug a huge *hole*. <u>count noun</u>

Chapter 18

18-2: Exercise 1: Finish the sentence. Start each *noun clause* with *whether* or *if*.

1. I don't know: <u>whether she lives in Ohio.</u>
2. I don't know: <u>if I'm going to the movies later.</u>
3. I don't know: <u>if she's a Native American.</u>
4. I don't know: <u>whether they'll go the restaurant later.</u>
5. I don't know: <u>whether Mike has an extra pencil.</u>
6. I don't know: <u>if Mike and Sam are still fighting.</u>
7. I don't know: <u>whether it will rain today.</u>
8. I don't know: <u>whether Thomas is still in the hospital.</u>
9. I don't know: <u>if we are still going to California.</u>
10. I don't know: <u>if she's hurt.</u>

18-3: Exercise 1: Complete the sentence with the correct *noun clause*.

1. I don't know: <u>where Tom lives.</u>
2. I don't know: <u>who's (who is) going to be at my party.</u>
3. I don't know: <u>how to make bread.</u>
4. I don't know: <u>when I am going to the supermarket.</u>
5. I don't know: <u>why she's cleaning.</u>
6. I know: <u>where Oregon is.</u>
7. I know: <u>who's (who is) at the door.</u>
8. I don't know: <u>how to ride a bike.</u>
9. I know: <u>when they are going to New York City.</u>
10. I know: <u>why she's laughing.</u>

18-4: Exercise 1: Rewrite each sentence placing the word *that* in the sentence.

1. I think <u>that</u> it definitely is.
2. I think <u>that</u> he's a great physician.
3. I think <u>that</u> it's pretty good.
4. I know <u>that</u> they're very large.
5. I think <u>that</u> it's a huge country.
6. I think <u>that</u> it's a beautiful language.
7. I think <u>that</u> he's real.
8. I think <u>that</u> he's difficult to understand also.

9. I think <u>that</u> it's a wonderful city to visit.
10. I don't. I think <u>that</u> their fake.

Chapter 19

19-1: Exercise 1: Using the choices in the box, fill in the blank with the correct *modal auxiliary*.

1. **Would** you go to the store and buy a pound of sugar?
2. I **can** name all fifty states alphabetically.
3. **May** I please borrow a pencil?
4. You **must** wear a jacket. It's freezing!
5. Jessica was full. She **could** not eat another bite.
6. Do I **have to** sit with Aunt Judy? She always teases me.
7. You **ought to** put more air in your front tire.
8. **Would** you please turn the music down?
9. **Shall** I call the nurse?
10. **Will** you please stop tapping your pencil on the desk?

19-1: Exercise 2: Rewrite each sentence using the statement provided and the *modal auxiliary* in parentheses.

1. (may) May I go to the restroom?
2. (ought to) You ought to read book.
3. (used to) I used to play the piano when I was five.
4. (will) I will clean my room before my parents get home.
5. (need) I need to find my retainer.
6. (shall) Shall we dance?
7. (could) You could take the bus to your house.
8. (can) I can juggle.
9. (must) You must brush your teeth every day.
10. (have to) You have to study.

19-2 through 19-4: Exercise 1: Underline the correct *modal* for each sentence.

1. (<u>Did you mind</u> / Can I) that I borrowed your pencil?
2. (Do you mind / <u>May I</u>) go to the restroom?
3. (<u>Can I</u> / Do you mind) have some candy?
4. (<u>Would you</u> / Do you mind) go to the post office?
5. (Do you / <u>Could you</u>) buy my lunch? I have no money.
6. (<u>Can you</u> / Do you) change the TV channel?
7. (<u>Would you</u> / can you) mind taking these books to the library?
8. (Can I / <u>Do you</u>) mind if I watch TV?
9. (<u>Can I</u> / Do you) go to the party on Saturday?
10. (Can I / <u>Would you</u>) mind taking the trash out?

19-5: Exercise 1: Underline the correct *verb* in each sentence that makes the most sense.

1. (<u>Walk</u> / Open) up the hill.
2. (Go / <u>Stop</u>) at the stop sign.
3. (<u>Mow</u> / Play) the lawn.
4. (See / <u>Walk</u>) faster.
5. (Live / <u>Open</u>) the door.
6. (<u>Drive</u> / Grow) slower.
7. (See / <u>Look</u>) at the time.
8. (<u>Write</u> / Kick) neater.
9. (Carry / <u>Run</u>) over there.
10. (Swim / <u>Dig</u>) into the ground.

Chapter 20

20-1: Exercise 1: Underline the correct *degree of certainty* for each sentence. Look at the percentage next to the question, then look above to match the *degree of certainty* with the percentage.

1. 60% → Terri (<u>could be</u> / must be) a girl's name.
2. 100% → My mom (maybe / <u>is</u>) a slow driver
3. 100% → My dad (<u>is</u> / must be) sick
4. 90% → Your shoes (<u>must be</u> / is) in the closet.
5. 100% → Tom (must be / <u>is</u>) sad.
6. 60% → John (<u>might be</u> / is) on time if he woke up early.
7. 100% → Seth (maybe / <u>is</u>) late
8. 100% → Ann (could be / <u>is</u>) at the store.
9. 60% → Chris (must be / <u>maybe</u>) at home.
10. 90% → Your keys (<u>must be</u> / are) on the table.

20-2: Exercise 1: Underline the correct *degree of certainty* for each sentence. Look at the percentage next to the question, then look above to match the *degree of certainty* with the percentage.

1. 100% → Mike (<u>isn't</u> / couldn't be) a girl's name.
2. 60% → Tom (must not be / <u>may not be</u>) with Mary.
3. 100% → My dad (<u>isn't</u> / must not be) sick.
4. 90% → Your shoes (are not / <u>couldn't be</u>) in the closet.
5. 100% → Tom (<u>isn't</u> / may not be) sad.
6. 60% → John (might not be / <u>must not be</u>) on time if he didn't wake up early.
7. 100% → Seth (<u>isn't</u> / may not be) late.
8. 100% → Ann (couldn't / <u>isn't</u>) at the store.
9. 60% → Jake (must not be / <u>may not be</u>) at home.
10. 90% → Your keys (isn't / <u>must not be</u>) on the table.

20-3: Exercise 1: Underline the correct *degree of certainty* for each sentence. Look at the percentage next to the question, then look above to match the *degree of certainty* with the percentage.

1. 100% → Terri (<u>was</u> / could have been) a girl's name.
2. 90% → My mom (<u>must have been</u> / was) a slow driver.
3. 80% → Your dad (must have been / <u>could have been</u>) sick.
4. 60% → Your shoes (<u>may have been</u> / must have been) in the closet.
5. 90% → Tom (may have been / <u>must have been</u>) sad.
6. 80% → John (might have been / <u>could have been</u>) on time if he woke up early.
7. 60% → Seth (was / <u>might have been</u>) late.
8. 100% → Ann (must have been / <u>was</u>) at the store.
9. 90% → Jake (<u>must have been</u> / may have been) at home.
10. 80% → Your keys (<u>could have been</u> / must have been) on the table.

20-4: Exercise 1: Underline the correct *degree of certainty* for each sentence. Look at the percentage next to the question, then look above to match the *degree of certainty* with the percentage.

1. 100% → Terri (<u>will be</u> / might be) at soccer practice.
2. 90% → She (will not be / <u>should not be</u>) at school. She's sick.
3. 100% → They (<u>will be</u> / might be) with her mother this weekend.
4. 60% → They (will be / <u>could be</u>) at the park.
5. 90% → Mike (could be / <u>should be</u>) at work.
6. 100% → John (<u>will be</u> / could be) at my house on Thursday.
7. 60% → Seth (might not be / <u>will not be</u>) on time for work. He is in traffic.
8. 100% → Ben (<u>will be</u> / should be) at the store.
9. 90% → Jake (<u>should be</u> / could be) at home by 9:00pm.
10. 80% → Your keys (will be / <u>might be</u>) on the table.

Chapter 22

22-1: Exercise 1: Write a complete sentence making a suggestion for what the person/people should do in each situation. *Note: These are example answers. Answers will vary.*

1. Why don't you make some macaroni and cheese?
2. Why don't you buy a blue car?
3. Why don't we get a job?
4. Why don't we buy tickets early?
5. Why don't we go to the beach tomorrow?
6. Why doesn't he write her a note?
7. Why doesn't he ask his mom for a loan?
8. Why doesn't she research careers online?
9. Why doesn't Emily go to the library?
10. Why not talk to your teacher?
11. Why don't you try selling them at school?

Chapter 23

23-2 through 23-2: Exercise 1: Underline the correct *coordinating conjunction*. There are five questions where both answer choices are correct. There are five questions where only <u>one</u> answer choice is correct.

1. He likes to run (<u>and</u> / <u>or</u>) exercise.
2. My mom drives slowly (<u>and</u> / <u>but</u>) carefully.
3. I don't like school, (<u>nor</u> / and) do I like sports.
4. She likes to read (<u>and</u> / nor) write.
5. I like John (<u>and</u> / <u>or</u>) Jack.
6. I went to Oregon (<u>and</u> / but) California.
7. I saw the *Batman* (<u>and</u> / or) *Indiana Jones* movies at the same time.
8. She likes books (<u>and</u> / <u>or</u>) music.
9. She has a cell phone (<u>and</u> / <u>or</u>) a laptop.
10. Eric bought a watch (but / <u>and</u>) a pair of shoes.

Chapter 24

24-1: Exercise 1: Underline the sentence that is grammatically correct?

1. B. <u>I can't go to any game.</u>
2. A. <u>I won't have any money.</u>
3. B. <u>I have no change.</u>
4. B. <u>She isn't going to take a shower.</u>
5. B. <u>They didn't read any books over the summer.</u>
6. B. <u>Tom doesn't have any paper; you must buy your own.</u>
7. A. <u>She doesn't have any money.</u>
8. B. <u>Mike can't get any sicker.</u>
9. B. <u>Ashley and Mike are not dating anymore.</u>
10. B. <u>I can't get any rest.</u>

Chapter 25

25-1: Exercise 1: The first sentence is *active*; the second sentence is *passive*. Change the *active* to the *passive* by underlining the correct form of *be*.

1. Sophia cleans the house every day.
   Every day, the house (<u>is being</u> / has been) cleaned by Sophia.
2. Sophia is cleaning the house.
   The house (<u>is being</u> / has been) cleaned by Sophia.
3. Sophia has cleaned the house.
   The house (is being / <u>has been</u>) cleaned by Sophia.
4. Sophia cleaned the house.
   The house (<u>was</u> / is) cleaned by Sophia.

5. Sophia was cleaning the house.
   The house (<u>was being</u> / has been) cleaned by Sophia.
6. Sophia had cleaned the house.
   The house (<u>had been</u> / has been) cleaned by Sophia.
7. Sophia will clean the house.
   The house (<u>will be</u> / is) cleaned by Sophia.
8. Sophia is going to clean the house.
   The house (<u>is going to be</u> / was) cleaned by Sophia.
9. Sophia will have cleaned the house.
   The house (<u>will have been</u> / was) cleaned by Sophia.

25-1: Exercise 2: Read the following sentences. If they are written in active voice, write *active*, if they are written in passive voice, write *passive*.

1. I have to help my sister with her homework. <u>active</u>
2. A new leash for the dog was given by my aunt. <u>passive</u>
3. The National Anthem was written by Francis Scott Key. <u>passive</u>
4. I am sitting by the lake. <u>active</u>
5. Chocolate ice cream was eaten by everyone at the party. <u>passive</u>
6. I stood next to the statue. <u>active</u>
7. Sabrina was making everyone dinner. <u>active</u>
8. The flu was passed from one classmate to another. <u>passive</u>
9. Tuna was fed to the cats. <u>passive</u>
10. The dishes were washed by Kelly. <u>passive</u>

Chapter 26

26-1 through 26-2: Exercise 1: Underline the correct form of *present tense* for the *conditional clauses*.

1. If I (<u>walk</u> / walked / will walk) to school, I usually (<u>take</u> / took / will take) the bus.
2. If I usually (<u>go</u> / will go / went) to school, I (took / <u>take</u> / will take) usually the bus.
3. If I (drank / <u>drink</u> / will drink) too much water, I have to (<u>go</u> / will go / went) to the bathroom.
4. If the dog (bit / <u>bites</u> / bited) a person, he has to (<u>go</u> / will go / went) to the animal shelter.
5. When I (washed / <u>wash</u> / will wash) my car, I usually (scrubbed / <u>scrub</u> / will scrub) the tires.
6. When Tom and Pat (<u>travel</u> / will travel / traveled) to California, they usually (<u>go</u> / went / will go) to Los Angles.
7. When the city of New York (<u>has</u> / have / will have) a parade, the city (closed / <u>close</u> / will close) the streets.
8. If I (<u>fail</u> / failed / will fail) this test, I (<u>start</u> / started / will start) crying.
9. When I (walked / will walk / <u>walk</u>) to the store, I usually (walked / will walk / <u>walk</u>) on the sidewalk.
10. If I don't (<u>do</u> / doing / done) my homework, my mother usually (yell / <u>yells</u> / yelling) at me.

26-3: Exercise 1: Underline the correct *verb* for the *past real conditional*.

1. When I (<u>had</u> / have / will have) a dollar, I used to (<u>spend</u> / spent / will spend) it. Now, I put the money in a savings bank account.
2. If I (<u>read</u> / red / will read) a long book in English, it used to (<u>be</u> / been / will be) difficult. Now, with practice, it's much easier.
3. When I (<u>had</u> / have / will have) to mow the grass, it usually (<u>took</u> / take / will took) me a long time. Now, I hire a person to cut the grass.
4. If I (run / <u>ran</u> / will run) a long distance, I usually (<u>took</u> / take / will took) a long time. Now, I can run marathon.
5. If the weather (is / <u>was</u> / were) good, I usually (<u>took</u> / take / will took) my dog on a walk.
6. When I (<u>had</u> / have / will have) to complete my school work, I often (forget / <u>forgot</u> / forgotten). Now, I am older and wiser.
7. When I (<u>had</u> / have / will have) an argument with my mother, I usually (get / <u>got</u> / gotten) upset. Now, I don't anymore.
8. I used to (<u>walk</u> / walked / will walk) to work every day. Now I drive.
9. When I was younger and I (get / <u>got</u> / gotten) invited to many parties, I usually (<u>took</u> / take / will took) a bottle of wine with me.
10. I used to (<u>drink</u> / drank / will drink) a lot, but now I don't (<u>drink</u> / drank / will drink) alcohol anymore.

26-4: Exercise 1: Underline the correct form of *future real conditional* for each sentence.

1. If I (<u>go</u> / gone / will go) to the gym tonight, I (<u>will need</u> / will needed / needed) a towel to go swimming.
2. If I (<u>drive</u> / will drive / will drove) to the store now, I (miss / missed / <u>will miss</u>) will my favorite television show.
3. When I (got / <u>get</u> / will got) some money, I'm (will buy / <u>going to buy</u> / bought) a new computer.
4. When the weather (get / <u>gets</u> / got) better, we will (<u>start</u> / started / starting) going to the beach.
5. If I can (<u>complete</u> / completing / completed) my homework, I'm (go / gone / <u>going</u>) to the park.
6. If I (<u>drive</u> / drove / driving) to California, I'm (<u>going</u> / going / gone) to take my wife with me.
7. When I (<u>go</u> / going / gone) to the movie theater, I will (<u>buy</u> / buying / bought) some candy.
8. If she does her (<u>work</u> / working / worked) poorly, I will have to (<u>ask</u> / asking / asked) her to do the work again.
9. If the book (are / <u>is</u>) too long, I will not (has / had / <u>have</u>) a chance to finish it.
10. When I get (<u>work</u> / working / worked) to this morning, I am (go / <u>going</u> / gone) to call my mother.

Chapter 27

27-1: Exercise 1: Underline the correct form of the *present unreal conditional*. Follow the sentence structure above to help you answer the questions.

1. If I (<u>start</u> / started / will start) working, I would (<u>buy</u> / bought /will buy) a car.
2. Tom would (<u>walk</u> / walked / will walk) if he hadn't (break / <u>broken</u> / will break) his leg.
3. If Ana (<u>begun</u> / begin / will begin) reading, she would (been / <u>be</u> / will be) better at English.
4. If the teacher (grade / <u>graded</u> / will grade) my test, I would know what grade I (get / <u>got</u> / will got) in my class.
5. If I (go / <u>went</u> / will go) to the movies, I would not (<u>do</u> / will do / done) well on my test.

27-1: Exercise 2: Underline the correct form of the *present unreal conditional*. Follow the sentence structure above to help you answer the questions.

1. **Question:** Who would you (<u>pick</u> / picked / will pick) if you (<u>go</u> / will go / went) to the school dance?
   Answer: I (<u>would pick</u> / picked / will pick) Ann or Emily.
2. **Question:** What would you (<u>buy</u> / will buy / bought) if you (have / <u>had</u> / will have) one million dollars?
   Answer: I would (<u>buy</u> / will buy / bought) a big house.
3. **Question:** What would you (done / will do / <u>do</u>) if your wallet (were / <u>was</u>) stolen?
   Answer: I would (<u>call</u> / called / will call) the police.
4. **Question:** Where would (<u>live</u> / lived / will live) if you came to the United States?
   Answer: I would (<u>live</u> / lived / will live) in Washington, DC.
5. **Question:** What car would you (bought / <u>buy</u> / will buy) if you could (bought / <u>buy</u> / will buy) any car in the world?
   Answer: I would (bought / <u>buy</u> / will buy) a Porsche.

27-2: Exercise 1: Underline the correct *past unreal conditional* form for each sentence.

1. If I had (be / <u>been</u> / being) smarter, I could have (be / <u>been</u> / being) accepted into Harvard.
2. If she had (be / <u>been</u> / being) faster, I would have (give / giving / <u>given</u>) her a better tip.
3. I would have (mow / mowing / <u>mowed</u>) the lawn quicker, if we (have / <u>had</u> / having) a better lawn mower.
4. Seth could have (win / winning / <u>won</u>) the race if he had (practice / <u>practiced</u> / practicing) more.
5. Susan would have (move / moving / <u>moved</u>), if she had (find / <u>found</u> / finding) a nice house.
6. If Mary would have (work / <u>worked</u> / working) hard, she might still (<u>have</u> / had / having) her job.
7. If Michael had been (pay / <u>paying</u> / paid) attention, he would have (get / got / <u>gotten</u>) a better grade on the test.
8. Ann would have (travel / traveling / <u>traveled</u>) to Paris if she could have (afford / affording / <u>afforded</u>) the plane ticket.

---

9. I would have (drive / <u>driven</u> / drove) to California, if gas had not (be / <u>been</u> / being) so expensive.
10. I could have (be / <u>been</u> / being) a famous musician if I would have (win / winning / <u>won</u>) American Idol.

27-3: Exercise 1: Underline the correct *future unreal conditional* form for each sentence.

1. If I (has / <u>had</u> / have) a good car, I would not have to worry about fixing it every day.
2. I would (<u>go</u> / going / gone) to New York right now, if I were on vacation.
3. If I were rich, I would be (travel / traveled / <u>traveling</u>) the world.
4. If I (has / <u>had</u> / have) a child, I would be a great parent.
5. If I were (go / <u>going</u> / gone) to California, it would be wonderful.
6. If I were not going to work, I would be (travel / traveled / <u>traveling</u>) to the beach.
7. If I had a good computer, I could (<u>complete</u> / completed / completing) my work faster.
8. I would (<u>go</u> / going / gone) to work today, if I wasn't sick.
9. If I were a famous actor, I would be (live / lived / <u>living</u>) in Hollywood.
10. If I were (move / moved / <u>moving</u>) to Washington, DC, my wife would be going with me.

Chapter 28

28-1: Exercise 1: Underline the correct *continuous conditional* form for each sentence.

1. She is (drive / <u>driving</u> / will drive) down the street.
2. If Ann is still (watch / watched / <u>watching</u>) television, I would (<u>ask</u> / asked / asking) her to help you.
3. If Tom is (do / <u>doing</u> / done) his homework, I would (<u>ask</u> / asked / asking) him to help you with yours.
4. If Jennifer is (practice / practiced / <u>practicing</u>) for the marathon, I would (<u>practice</u> / practiced / practicing) with her.
5. If she had been (pay / paid / <u>paying</u>) attention in class, she would (<u>have</u> / has / had) gotten an "A" on her test.
6. If the dog (have / has / <u>had</u>) been at home, he could have (stop / <u>stopped</u> / stopping) the thief from coming in the house.
7. If Mike had been (listen / listened / <u>listening</u>), he would have (hear / hearing / <u>heard</u>) the teacher give the directions.
8. If I were (study / <u>studying</u> / studied) English in the United States, I would (<u>quit</u> / quitting) my job tomorrow.
9. If I were (make / <u>making</u> / made) a lot of money, I would (<u>buy</u> / buying / bought) a big house for my family and myself.
10. If I were (speak / <u>speaking</u> / spoken) English, I would try and (<u>ask</u> / asked / asking) my boss for more money.

28-2: Exercise 1: Underline the correct *mixed conditional* for each sentence.

1. If I (was / <u>were</u> / am) more athletic, I would be a marathon runner.
2. If I had (finish / <u>finished</u> / finishing) the book, I would be going to the book discussion tonight.
3. If I (aren't / <u>weren't</u> / am) running the marathon this Fall, I would have eaten more desserts at dinner.
4. If you were bilingual, I would (<u>send</u> / sent / sended) you to the conference in New York City.
5. If I (was practiced / <u>had practiced</u> / am practiced) longer, I would be a lot better at playing my guitar.
6. If I weren't leaving for Paris, I would have (buyed / <u>bought</u> / buy) that apartment.
7. If I weren't driving to my parents' house this weekend, I (<u>would work</u> / would worked / were work) on my project for school.
8. If I had (drink / <u>drank</u> / drunk) that spoiled milk, I would be very sick now.
9. If they weren't talking so much, they (would have here / would have hear / <u>would have heard</u>) the directions.
10. If they had stopped at the stoplight, they would not be (ask / asked / <u>asking</u>) the police officer for forgiveness.

28-3: Exercise 1: Underline the correct *verb* form for each *were to conditional* sentence.

1. If I were to (<u>see</u> / saw / seen) a ghost, I would be so scared.
2. If the tornado were to have (destroy / destroying / <u>destroyed</u>) the school, the people of the city would be very upset.
3. If I were to (<u>get</u> / got / gotten) an "A" on my test, my mom will allow me to out with my friends tonight.
4. If someone were to (has / <u>have</u> / had) nice car we could borrow, tonight would be perfect.
5. If the computer were to (broke / <u>break</u> / broken) down, I would lose all of my work.
6. If my cell phone were to (<u>go</u> / going /gone) off in the middle of the exam, I would be so embarrassed.
7. If we were to (has / <u>have</u> / had) an earthquake, the city would be in panic.
8. Question: Did you study for the test tomorrow?
   Answer: No, but if I were to (<u>study</u> / studying / studied) tonight, for the whole test, I may pass.
9. If I were to (<u>pass</u> / passing / passed) my driving test tomorrow, I will finally have my driver's license.
10. If I were to (<u>cook</u> / cooking / cooked) you dinner tonight, you must wash the dishes.

Index

www.ingramcontent.com/pod-product-compliance
Lightning Source LLC
LaVergne TN
LVHW061222060426
835509LV00012B/1384